Current
CONTROVERSIES

Freedom of Speech on Campus

Other Books in the Current Controversies Series

Freedom of Speech on Campus

Eamon Doyle, Book Editor

GREENHAVEN
PUBLISHING

Published in 2019 by Greenhaven Publishing, LLC
353 3rd Avenue, Suite 255, New York, NY 10010

Copyright © 2019 by Greenhaven Publishing, LLC

First Edition

Articles in Greenhaven Publishing anthologies are often edited for length to meet page
requirements. In addition, original titles of these works are changed to clearly present
the main thesis and to explicitly indicate the author's opinion. Every effort is made to
ensure that Greenhaven Publishing accurately reflects the original intent of the authors.
Every effort has been made to trace the owners of the copyrighted material.

Cover image: Mario Tama/Getty Images

Library of Congress Cataloging-in-Publication Data
Names: Doyle, Eamon, editor.
Title: Freedom of speech on campus / Eamon Doyle, Editor.
Description: New York : Greenhaven Publishing, 2018. | Series: Current
  controversies | Includes bibliographical references and index. | Audience: Grades 9–12.
Identifiers: LCCN 2018001056| ISBN 9781534503076 (library bound) | ISBN
  9781534503083 (pbk.)
Subjects: LCSH: Freedom of speech—United States—Juvenile literature. |
  College students—Legal status, laws, etc.—United States—Juvenile
  literature. | College students—Civil rights—United States—Juvenile
  literature.
Classification: LCC KF4772 .F7435 2018 | DDC 323.44/30973—dc23
LC record available at https://lccn.loc.gov/2018001056

Manufactured in the United States of America

Website: http://greenhavenpublishing.com

Contents

Chapter 1: Are University Campuses Biased Against Conservative Viewpoints?

Colin Barker

Since the Vietnam War and the student protests of the 1960s, the university campus has functioned as an emblem of the liberal-conservative and rural-urban divisions in American culture.

Yes: University Campuses Threaten Free Speech Through Bias Against Conservative Viewpoints

Nat Hentoff

Recent examples of free speech–related conflicts illustrate an increasingly pronounced pattern of active hostility toward free speech on college campuses.

Daniel Jacobson

Intellectual arguments that question the viability and value of free speech do not hold up and represent a threat to the classical liberal values that have shaped modern democracy.

Nancy Thorner and Bonnie O'Neil

Only a small percentage of academics identify as conservative, and professors encourage students to adopt their own liberal perspective on important issues. This has created an environment on campus that is hostile to conservative viewpoints and, by extension, to free speech rights in general.

No: Conservative Anxieties About Liberal-Dominated Campuses Are Overblown

Chapter 2: Should First Amendment Protections Extend to All Speech?

to suppress speech that is deemed offensive to the cultural identity of its members as a means of protecting them from the impact of prejudice.

Yes: Free Speech Rights Must Be Absolute

Anthony D. Romero

Free speech rights are so critical from a legal and civil liberties perspective that organizations like the ACLU, which publicly and unequivocally rejects racist and white supremacist ideology, have rightly defended the free speech rights of Nazis and the Ku Klux Klan.

Robert Jensen

The life of Scott Nearing, an early twentieth-century American teacher and writer, exemplifies the potential destructiveness of limits on free speech in an academic setting.

No: Some Types of Speech Need to Be Restricted

Traci Yoder

Part of maintaining a civil, well-ordered culture involves enforcing certain norms of behavior and conversation. Some types of hateful or subversive speech represent a threat to our civil order and should be suppressed.

Elizabeth Dovell

Hate speech is often symptomatic of toxic underlying social dynamics (such as racism, homophobia, and bigotry) that, left unaddressed, can lead to violence or even genocide.

Chapter 3: Does Some Hate Speech Qualify as a Type of Violence?

Joyce Arthur and Peter Tatchell

Liberal critical theorists have advocated for a more diffuse conception of cultural oppression, introducing concepts like microaggressions. Students at a number of institutions have demanded various new protections, including "safe spaces" and "trigger warnings." In response, free speech absolutists have decried political correctness run amok, portraying college campuses as a liberal assault on free speech.

Yes: The Trauma That Hostile Words Inflict on Marginalized Groups Can Qualify as Violence

Aaron Moritz

There is no significant difference between types of harm, and attempting to find them ignores the issue at hand. Hate speech is a type of violence and we should be able to regulate it the same way that we regulate other violent crimes.

Barrett Holmes Pitner

The United States can learn something from countries like Canada and Germany, whose free speech restrictions reflect a stronger understanding of the historical dangers of certain types of free speech.

No: The Distinction Between Speech and Physical Violence Supports Free Expression

Nadine Strossen and Tom Patterson

The tendency for universities to treat all types of sexually themed expression, including speech that is not targeted at a particular individual, as sexual harassment threatens important academic discourse and distracts from the pressing issues of sexual assault and violence. Teaching students how to distinguish between offensive speech and actual violence and how to engage in discourses that may contain offensive viewpoints is essential to the future protection of free speech.

Josh Craddock

Intellectual challenges to the distinction between speech and violence, currently prevalent among academics who subscribe to Judith Butler, involve a radical and unmerited expansion of the respective definitions of "stress," "power," and "violence."

Chapter 4: Should Speech on Campus Be Regulated More Than Other Public Speech?

Mary Ellen Flannery

The conflict between free speech absolutists and skeptics has reached a fever pitch and, given the complexity and sensitivity of the issues involved, it may be necessary to create some type of national task force to examine issues of free speech, discrimination, and harassment on campus.

Yes: Restrictions on Offensive Speech May Help Universities Create a Positive Atmosphere of Free Inquiry

Scott Bomboy

Universities should be able to enforce certain speech norms to maintain the stability of their community, which is composed of individuals from all types of cultural and economic backgrounds.

PEN America

The US Department of Education's current policies on harassment and offensive speech exemplify how certain restrictions on speech can support minority groups and other vulnerable persons' feelings of safety and acceptance within a community.

No: Citizens Do Not Shed Their First Amendment Protections When They Walk Onto a University Campus

Foreword

"Controversy" is a word that has an undeniably unpleasant connotation. It carries a definite negative charge. Controversy can spoil family gatherings, spread a chill around classroom and campus discussions, inflame public discourse, open raw civic wounds, and lead to the ouster of public officials. We often feel that controversy is almost akin to bad manners, a rude and shocking eruption of that which must not be spoken or thought of in polite, tightly guarded society. To avoid controversy, to quell controversy, is often seen as a public good, a victory for etiquette, perhaps even a moral or ethical imperative.

Yet the studious, deliberate avoidance of controversy is also a whitewashing, a denial, a death threat to democracy. It is a false sterilizing and sanitizing and superficial ordering of the messy, ragged, chaotic, at times ugly processes by which a healthy democracy identifies and confronts challenges, engages in passionate debate about appropriate approaches and solutions, and arrives at something like a consensus and a broadly accepted and supported way forward. Controversy is the megaphone, the speaker's corner, the public square through which the citizenry finds and uses its voice. Controversy is the life's blood of our democracy and absolutely essential to the vibrant health of our society.

Our present age is certainly no stranger to controversy. We are consumed by fierce debates about technology, privacy, political correctness, poverty, violence, crime and policing, guns, immigration, civil and human rights, terrorism, militarism, environmental protection, and gender and racial equality. Loudly competing voices are raised every day, shouting opposing opinions, putting forth competing agendas, and summoning starkly different visions of a utopian or dystopian future. Often these voices attempt to shout the others down; there is precious little listening and considering among the cacophonous din. Yet listening and considering, too, are essential to the health of a democracy. If controversy is democracy's lusty lifeblood, respectful listening and careful thought are its higher faculties, its brain, its conscience.

Current Controversies does not shy away from or attempt to hush the loudly competing voices. It seeks to provide readers with as wide and representative as possible a range of articulate voices on any given controversy of the day, separate each one out to allow it to be heard clearly and fairly, and encourage careful listening to each of these well-crafted, thoughtfully expressed opinions, supplied by some of today's leading academics, thinkers, analysts, politicians, policy makers, economists, activists, change agents, and advocates. Only after listening to a wide range of opinions on an issue, evaluating the strengths and weaknesses of each argument, assessing how well the facts and available evidence mesh with the stated opinions and conclusions, and thoughtfully and critically examining one's own beliefs and conscience can the reader begin to arrive at his or her own conclusions and articulate his or her own stance on the spotlighted controversy.

This process is facilitated and supported in each Current Controversies volume by an introduction and chapter overviews that provide readers with the essential context they need to begin engaging with the spotlighted controversies, with the debates surrounding them, and with their own perhaps shifting or nascent opinions on them. Chapters are organized around several key questions that are answered with diverse opinions representing all points on the political spectrum. In its content, organization, and methodology, readers are encouraged to determine the authors' point of view and purpose, interrogate and analyze the various arguments and their rhetoric and structure, evaluate the arguments' strengths and weaknesses, test their claims against available facts and evidence, judge the validity of the reasoning, and bring into clearer, sharper focus the reader's own beliefs and conclusions and how they may differ from or align with those in the collection or those of classmates.

Research has shown that reading comprehension skills improve dramatically when students are provided with compelling, intriguing, and relevant "discussable" texts. The subject matter of these collections could not be more compelling, intriguing, or urgently relevant to today's students and the world they are poised to inherit. The anthologized articles also provide the basis for stimulating, lively, and passionate classroom debates. Students who are compelled to anticipate objections to their own argument and identify the flaws in those of an opponent read more carefully, think more critically, and steep themselves in relevant context, facts, and information more thoroughly. In short, using discussable text of the kind provided by every single volume in the Current Controversies series encourages close reading, facilitates reading comprehension, fosters research, strengthens critical thinking, and greatly enlivens and energizes classroom discussion and participation. The entire learning process is deepened, extended, and strengthened.

If we are to foster a knowledgeable, responsible, active, and engaged citizenry, we must provide readers with the intellectual, interpretive, and critical-thinking tools and experience necessary to make sense of the world around them and of the all-important debates and arguments that inform it. We must encourage them not to run away from or attempt to quell controversy but to embrace it in a responsible, conscientious, and thoughtful way, to sharpen and strengthen their own informed opinions by listening to and critically analyzing those of others. This series encourages respectful engagement with and analysis of current controversies and competing opinions and fosters a resulting increase in the strength and rigor of one's own opinions and stances. As such, it helps readers assume their rightful place in the public square and provides them with the skills necessary to uphold their awesome responsibility—guaranteeing the continued and future health of a vital, vibrant, and free democracy.

Introduction

> *"Freedom of speech is a principal*
> *pillar of a free government: When*
> *this support is taken away, the*
> *constitution of a free society*
> *is dissolved."*
>
> *-Benjamin Franklin*

Free speech rights are widely considered to be one of the essential differences between democratic and authoritarian forms of governance. In the United States, the right to free speech is established in the First Amendment to the US Constitution, the interpretation of which has been the subject of legal and political debates (including important Supreme Court cases such as *Shenck v. United States* (1919) and *Brandenburg v. Ohio* (1969)) throughout the country's history. Some of the most controversial issues focus specifically on the right to various types of public protest, such as flag burning, picketing, and street demonstrations; others relate more to defamation, harassment, and hate speech.

In the 1960s, student protests against the Vietnam War (1955-1975) marked the college campus as an important First Amendment battleground and a symbol of the political divisions in American society.[1] Conservatives worried that the protests were using free speech rights as a cover to create mischief and spread seditious, unpatriotic ideas; liberals, on the other hand, viewed the protests as an expression of democratic ideals. In the decades since, the enmity that emerged between liberals and conservatives over the issue of Vietnam War protests has shaped debates on the role of campus culture, the purpose of higher education, and the distinction between free speech and hate speech.

In recent years, the college campus has found itself once again at the center of First Amendment debates. This time, the controversy has more to do with hate speech, discrimination against minority groups, and new forms of identity politics that question the wisdom of absolute free speech rights. Campus activists argue that American society as a whole is entirely saturated with inequality, prejudice, and discrimination, and that they are fighting to create space on campus for marginalized groups to find reprieve from an environment of injustice and hostility. Student activists have protested against—and in some cases attempted to shut down—guest speakers with views deemed insensitive or politically incorrect. They have adopted the rhetoric of liberal critical theorists like Judith Butler, who have attempted to cast hate speech as indistinct from physical violence. At some schools, students have demanded that professors offer "trigger warnings" before presenting controversial material with the potential to offend or upset.

Conservatives and organizations dedicated to promoting an absolutist interpretation of free speech rights (such as the American Civil Liberties Union) have largely recoiled from these developments, characterizing campus activists as hysterical and un-American in their skepticism of the country's robust free speech tradition. They argue that free speech rights are inherently and necessarily absolute when properly interpreted. They claim that college campuses are no different in this regard than any other class of institution in America, and should be accorded no unique status with regard to the First Amendment. From this perspective (exemplified in the following quotation by Jeffrey Herbst of the Newseum Institute), the ideological homogeneity of campus culture and students' hostility toward viewpoints that diverge from a specific set of multicultural liberal orthodoxies has become a threat to free speech rights in general:

College campuses should be bastions of free speech. Today, they often seem to be the very places in American society where there is the least tolerance for controversial ideas. Unfortunately, much of the discussion of why this has occurred is based on the ad hoc experiences of a few campuses that briefly gained national attention when lecturers were harassed or prevented from speaking by unruly and, occasionally, riotous crowds. Systematic public opinion polling and anecdotal evidence suggests, however, that the real problem of free expression on college campuses is much deeper than episodic moments of censorship: With little comment, an alternate understanding of the First Amendment has emerged among young people that can be called "the right to non-offensive speech." This perspective essentially carves out an exception to the right of free speech by trying to prevent expression that is seen as particularly offensive to an identifiable group, especially if that collective is defined in terms of race, ethnicity, gender, or sexual identity.[2]

To support their view, writers like Herbst point to the low percentage of academics who identify as conservative and to polling data demonstrating increased skepticism[3] among college students about the value of free speech rights.

On the other side, some educators, students, and writers have suggested that portrayals of a campus culture hostile to conservatives are wildly overblown and that there are valid reasons to limit certain types of speech, particularly in unique environments like the modern university campus:

The ACLU and many liberal-minded people assume that allowing all speech under any circumstances will ensure that the best ideas win out and that it is ideal to have even potentially dangerous ideas out in the open where they can be challenged. They question attempts by universities to adopt codes and policies prohibiting hate speech, arguing that this well-intentioned response is incorrect and akin to censorship. [...] If all sides are debated openly, advocates of this perspective contend, the best one will obviously succeed. However, far right conservative and fascist ideology is not simply based on logical and reasonable arguments; rather, these movements depend on the irrational mobilization of hate, fear, and anger against some of the most marginalized and vulnerable populations. Offering them an open forum and vigorously defending their right to promote harmful speech confers legitimacy on their positions as being equally as acceptable as any other.[4]

From this perspective, the ethnic and cultural diversity of their communities and the relative youth, inexperience, and vulnerability of students necessitates that university administrators take specific action to limit certain types of hostile and offensive speech. Rather than a threat to free expression, such efforts should be understood as a way to promote an atmosphere of free and inclusive inquiry.

Wherever the current debates lead, the college campus is likely to remain at the center of discussions about free speech in America for years to come. *Current Controversies: Freedom of Speech on Campus* will introduce readers to the range of perspectives surrounding this issue, helping them better understand the strong relationship between campus speech and free speech in general.

Endnotes

1. "Some Reflections on Student Movements of the 1960s and Early 1970s," by Colin Barker, Revues.org.

2. "Addressing the Real Crisis of Free Expression on Campus," by Jeffrey Herbst, Newseum Institute, April 25, 2017

3. Rampell, Catherine. "A Chilling Study Shows How Hostile College Students are Toward Free Speech," The *Washington Post.* September 18, 2017.

4. "Free Speech on Campus: A Critical Analysis," by Traci Yoder, National Lawyers Guild, May 25, 2017.

CHAPTER 1

Are University Campuses Biased Against Conservative Viewpoints?

The University Campus Has Been an Emblem of the Liberal-Conservative Divide Since the Student Protests of the 1960s

Colin Barker

Colin Barker is a sociologist and historian. He was a senior lecturer in Sociology at Manchester Metropolitan University from 1967 to 2002.

The Beginning, Berkeley 1964[1]

At the start of the fall term in 1964, student activists, some of whom had been involved in Freedom Summer and other civil rights activities, set up information tables on the street outside the Berkeley campus of the University of California, soliciting donations and supporters for civil rights causes. On September 14, 1964, Dean Katherine Towle announced that, since the strip of land where the tables were set up belonged to the University, the tables were banned under existing University regulations. These prohibited advocacy of political causes or candidates, outside political speakers, recruitment of members, and fundraising by student organizations, anywhere on the university campus. The rules, she declared, would be "strictly enforced." There were public confrontations at the tables between the university authorities and, among others, Mario Savio and Jack Weinberg, who won audiences when they spoke in defence of free speech. On 1st October, Weinberg was arrested and placed in a police car in Sproul Plaza, inside the university area. Inspired by ideas from the civil rights movement, several thousand students sat down around the car, trapping it (and its occupants) for the next 36 hours. Speakers climbed on top of the police car to address the large crowd in a permanent public meeting. The police charges against Weinberg were eventually dropped, and he was released.

A month later, however, the university brought its own disciplinary charges against those who organized the Sproul

Plaza sit-in. The Free Speech Movement, as it was now called, responded with an occupation of Sproul Hall, an administration building. The university called in the cops, and on the night of 3rd December some 800 students were carried from the Hall to waiting paddy-wagons. The continuing crisis in the university led to the appointment of a new acting chancellor, who introduced new rules for on-campus political activity, including the designation of the steps to Sproul Hall as an area where political tables could now be set up and speeches made. The campus movement had secured a significant victory over a conservative administration, though the issues rumbled on into the spring, involving conflicts with the University of California as a whole, and its Regents.[2]

Heirich comments that there seemed to be a 'kaleidoscope of crises', involving seven more collective confrontations in the spring of 1965, in whose course the targets and foci of conflict kept shifting.

> With each shift in the focus of conflict, issues became more difficult to meet directly and to resolve—both because they were more general and because they came closer to the heart of genuine value dilemmas that higher education had failed to solve in its massive growth over the preceding twenty-five years. (Heirich, 1970; Weinberg, 1965)

At each stage, different levels of authority in the university were challenged: from the student affairs staff to the deans, and then to the president and chancellor and then to the Regents. When the state Governor intervened, he was challenged by a university-wide strike. At each stage, the involvement of further authorities meant that a wider range of university relationships came into question, and under the students' critical surveillance.

Weinberg points out that the civil rights campaign tables were not just aimed at racism in the Deep South, but at the practices and interests of powerful local employers in the Bay Area. Those interests, he suggests, pressured the university, which succumbed. In that sense, many conclude that the FSM is an extension of the civil rights movement... The University of California is a microcosm in which all of the problems of our society are reflected. Not only did the pressure to crack down on free speech at Cal come from the outside power structure, but most of the failings of the university are either on-campus manifestations of broader American social problems or are imposed upon the university by outside pressures. (Weinberg, 1965).

Draper comments on the whole process:

One of the most unique features of the Berkeley student revolt is that from its beginning to its climax it was linked closely to the social and political issues and forces of the bigger society outside the campus. At every step the threads ran plainly to every facet of the social system: there were overt roles played by big business, politicians, government leaders, labor, the press, etc., as well as the Academy itself. This was no conflict in the cloister. (Draper, 1965)

The broadening of the conflicts meant that the nature of the university as an institution came increasingly into question, along with its linkages to the national and state-wide power structure. All of this tended to radicalize sections of the student body.

The very title of the movement, the Free Speech Movement, indicates the initial battle-ground between university authorities and students. Similar issues would resonate through later campus movements too. As an issue, 'freedom of speech' possessed a large mobilizing capacity. Previous civil rights activity, both in the Deep South but also in the San Francisco Bay area, had already habituated quite large numbers of Berkeley students to organized collective action.[3] The protest at Berkeley was not simply led by 'radicals', but by a coalition that included quite diverse political forces: civil rights campaigners, radical, socialist and peace groups, but also the Young Democrats and all three Republican Clubs including the right-wing Youth for Goldwater (Draper, 1965: 31-2).[4] There was something seemingly 'nonideological' about the student demands, which accounts in part for the very explosiveness of the student uprising: 'This was the explosiveness of uncalculated indignation, not the slow boil of planned revolt [...] the first discovery of the chasm between the rhetoric of Ideals and the cynicism of Power among the pillars of society' (Draper, *apud* Harman, 1988: 44). On the other hand, the very fact that the coalition was so broad meant that it could, and did, easily fracture and disassemble almost as quickly as it was formed. Nonetheless, what Berkeley showed was that an initially small group of students could, faced with a university administration that lumbered into action almost unaware of the sleeping energies its own responses could provoke, convert relatively small oppositional forces on a campus into a broad and wide-ranging student movement. If such movements lacked much by way of overall 'staying power', they were nonetheless, in the 1960s, an entirely novel development.[5] They also provided a kind of political 'forcing house' in which numbers of the student participants became, through their experiences within the movement and the exposure this gave them to radical critiques of existing society, much more ready to engage in wider radical politics.

Hal Draper, himself a librarian at Berkeley, was one of the few ideologically formed socialists in the faculty who supported the students from the beginning. His critique of Clark Kerr's ideas was very influential among the students who played a leading part in the early stages of the Berkeley movement.[6] In the book he published in 1965, he attempted a political anatomy of the newly emerged generation of student radicals. If they were not, as he put it, 'finished radicals', they had identified themselves as radical rather than liberal. Still in the early stages of a *process* of radicalization, they tended to concentrate on the 'issues' and to be more certain what they were against than what they were for. Among them '[...] the reservoir of radical energies is greater than the stream of radical beliefs'. Their overt thinking was marked by a conscious avoidance of any particular radical *ideology*. Disinclined to generalize and systematize their positions, they preferred to be 'pragmatic', inclining to substitute a 'moral' approach for political and social analysis.[7] He may well have had in mind a leading figure like Mario Savio, whose speech to students as they prepared to occupy Sproul Hall was reproduced all over the USA:

> There's a time when the operation of the machine becomes so odious, makes you so sick at heart, that you can't take part, you can't even passively take part, and you've got to put your bodies upon the gears and upon the wheels, upon the levers, upon all the apparatus, and you've got to make it stop! And you've got to indicate to the people who run it, to the people who own it, that unless you're free, the machine will be prevented from working at all! (cited in http://en.wikipedia.org/wiki/Mario_Savio)

Draper cited several reasons for the Berkeley students' rejection of 'ideology': they were rejecting *old* ideologies, not yet having met any new ideology that might carry them away; they feared ideological clarity might threaten the unity of their movement; and the general political climate of mid-1960s America made them refuse labels like 'socialist'. Their position had some advantages, in that it was harder to smear them with being 'communists'. The very unformed character of their ideas contributed to the explosiveness of their movements, indeed they lacked the kind of 'theoretical wisdom' that told them they couldn't win: a degree of naiveté and inexperience were as 'shield and buckler' to the student movement. At the same time, ideological weaknesses meant that they were ill-equipped to answer questions about what to do *next* after mass mobilizations had been achieved. Such movements could be tamed quite easily if the authorities recovered their poise and offered compromises that would quieten things down. They were liable to lack persistency in struggle, so the movements could rise and fade away with equal facility. 'The simple/moral drive to action' is more ephemeral than the ideological.' (Draper, 1965: 156-166).

If Draper was at one immensely enthusiastic, and sceptical, about the potential of movements like those at Berkeley, he was analyzing a situation *in statu nascendi*, not knowing how it might develop.[8] In the event, the Berkeley events did not immediately set off a rash of campus challenges to university authorities. In the United States, at least, other forms of student politics began to gain momentum. The American war in Vietnam slowly emerged as a core issue. Initially, the anti-war movement was tiny, but it grew through the new device of "teach-ins" on many campuses, beginning at Ann Arbor, Michigan in 1965. The teach-ins provided Marxists with an audience they'd not enjoyed for many years: audiences of thousands listened to Isaac Deutscher in Washington and to Hal Draper at Berkeley, as they debated with government spokespeople and largely won the arguments. Later that year the anti-war demonstrations started to gain serious momentum (Harman, 1988: 72). In turn, they fed back into campus radicalism, not only in the US, but in Europe.

Notes

1. There's an extensive collection of documents, photographs and other materials from the Berkeley Free Speech Movement on the web at http://www.fsm-a.org/.

2. The Regents commissioned a report into the causes of the unrest at Berkeley, which was scathing about the university administration: 'The University [...] displayed a consistent tendency to disorder its own principles and values. While dedicated to the maintenance of a house for ideas and thought, it proved selective in determining whose ideas would gain admittance. While upholding the value of a continuing discourse in the academic community, it refused to engage in simple conversation with the membership of that community. While positioned as the defender of man's right to reason, it acted out of fear that a volatile public would react against the University if exposed to the reasonings of students. While championing the value of the individual and his responsibility for his own person, it had sought to prevent the individual from suffering the consequences of his own self-determined actions in society. While postured to avoid prejudgment of the facts, it sought to determine before the fact the legality or illegality of actions students would plan to take in the surrounding community. While responsible to and for itself, the University assumed it would be charged with responsibility for others, and in fear that the assumption would prove valid, established rules prohibiting others form acting on their own responsibility' (The Byrne Report, cited in Draper, 1965: 237).

3. In March 1964, more than nine hundred people had been arrested during demonstrations at the Sheraton-Palace Hotel in San Francisco, including some two hundred from Berkeley (Heirich, 1970: 45). According to one study, more than half of those who sat down round the police car in Berkeley plaza had taken part in at least one civil rights protest, and 17 per cent had participated in seven or more (Lipset and Altbach, 1967: 202). Savio claimed that over 10 per cent of the Berkeley student body had taken part directly in civil rights activity, in the South or in the Bay Area (Draper, 1965: 3).

4. At the London School of Economics in 1967, the motion to occupy the college premises was moved by the former chair of the Conservative Society (Harman, 1988: 43).

5. Two American academics noted: 'Recent events in American student political life have shown that it is possible to remove students from their liberal but generally apathetic tendencies during a crisis. When the chips are down, as they were in Berkeley, a large proportion of the students supported the militants of the Free Speech Movement, even though the overwhelming majority did not normally take part in politics and have not remained active in the student movement. Similarly, such students will back a movement for civil rights in the campus community.' (Lipset and Altbach, 1967: 237-8)

6. Draper was the second speaker from the roof of the police car in Sproul Plaza, after Mario Savio.

7. Heirich has some materials from student essays about why they decided to join the FSM. They mix together moral arguments and beliefs, tactical commitments, a sense that the movement had generalized beyond a few radicals behind tables, expectations of success, and having friends who were participating (Heirich, 1970: 180-1).

8. Draper was to offer his own views about left strategy, arguing that the movement, to make lasting gains and develop ideological clarity, should 'lay new track'—to the American working class (Johnson, 1997).

There Is an Increasingly Pronounced Pattern of Hostility Toward Free Speech on American College Campuses

Nat Hentoff

Nat Hentoff was a columnist and staff writer with the Village Voice *for 51 years, from 1957 until 2008, and was one of the country's foremost authorities on the First Amendment. He earned numerous awards and was a widely acknowledged defender of civil liberties.*

Hostility to the exercise of free speech on American college campuses is nothing new. But what happened at Yale University, the University of Missouri and other colleges over the past two weeks is something new and frightening. The suppression of speech in academia has begun to spiral out of control.

Nicholas Christakis is a professor at Yale who lives with his wife in a student residence hall on campus. An internationally renowned physician and sociologist, Dr. Christakis was surrounded by dozens of angry students who showered him with curses and threats. Dr. Christakis' offense? He refused to publicly apologize for his wife's email that defended free speech and urged tolerance of offensive Halloween costumes.

Greg Lukianoff, the President of the Foundation for Individual Rights in Education (FIRE), was on the Yale campus to attend a free speech symposium and witnessed the incident. In the video Lukianoff posted on FIRE's website, Christakis appears on the verge of being physically assaulted.

"Nicholas addressed the crowd for more than an hour, even after it became clear that nothing short of begging for forgiveness would satisfy them," Lukianoff wrote in the *Washington Post.* "I've witnessed some intense campus disputes during my 14 years fighting for free speech, but nothing like this."

"Suppression of Free Speech in Academia Is Out of Control," by Nat Hentoff, Cato Institute, November 18, 2015. Reprinted by permission.

The next evening—at a William F. Buckley, Jr. Program conference on free speech that had been planned months in advance—Greg Lukianoff's speech was interrupted by a student who rushed the podium, shouting, before he was dragged out of the building by campus police. Attendees then braved a gauntlet of angry Yale students who cursed and ridiculed them. The *Yale Daily News* reported that "several attendees were spat on as they left."

At the University of Missouri, a student photographer freelancing for ESPN was confronted by a mob of angry anti-racism protesters who tried to eject him from the public commons area where they had gathered. After he refused to leave, the students begin a coordinated effort to both psychologically and physically intimidate the reporter into leaving.

The protesters subjected him to intense ridicule, sometimes chanting in unison, as they gradually forced him backwards. They then began to falsely accuse the reporter of the very conduct that they themselves were directing against him.

MU's student body vice president later tried to justify the students' self-imposed restrictions on the press during an interview on MSNBC. She suggested that the First Amendment "creates a hostile and unsafe learning environment."

Later that same week, a Christian street preacher, speaking within the campus "free speech circle," was physically assaulted and had his microphone appropriated by an anti-racism protester.

At Amherst College, a student group called Amherst Uprising issued a list of demands to administrators that included individual public apologies for what they claimed was a hostile environment of ethnocentric racism on campus. The list also included a demand for a written statement from administrators acknowledging that students who distribute leaflets defending free speech rights are subject to disciplinary action for being "racially insensitive," and that any students disciplined for such an offense must "attend extensive training for racial and cultural competency."

At Cornell, a well-meaning white student was forced to issue a public apology after he scheduled his own anti-racism protest without first getting the approval of the Black Student Union. He was accused, in multiple social media posts, of mocking the efforts of the BSU.

One commentator put him on notice that "if you are to be in (sic) ally, you have to acknowledge what you've done to hurt us." Within hours of scheduling the event, the offending student canceled the protest and issued a public apology thanking his critics "for calling me out on my ignorance."

These are not isolated incidents, but represent the organized adoption of mass public shaming tactics. Mass public shaming— traditionally used by autocratic regimes to silence their critics— is a particularly insidious form of censorship. It is designed to chill future speech by humiliating the speaker. Psychological manipulation and intimidation are used to impose forced speech as a means of social control.

Universities in the United States should not tolerate or appease such public shaming techniques. In his March 20, 2015, *New York Times* op-ed, "China's Tradition of Public Shaming Thrives," author Murong Xuecun writes that "cases of public shaming show us how in the name of some great cause, individual rights, dignity and privacy can all be sacrificed."

President Obama recently offered some advice to students and faculty who feel that the First Amendment creates a hostile and unsafe learning environment.

"You don't have to be fearful of somebody spouting bad ideas." Obama said during an interview last Sunday on ABC News. "Just out-argue them. Beat 'em. Make the case as to why they're wrong. Win over adherents. That's how things work in a democracy."

Intellectual Arguments That Question the Viability and Value of Free Speech Do Not Hold Up

Daniel Jacobson

Daniel Jacobson is a professor of philosophy at the University of Michigan. He has studied a range of topics in moral and political philosophy and held fellowships from the Princeton University Center for Human Values and the National Endowment for the Humanities.

Freedom of speech has been severely criticized at many American universities. Meanwhile, such prestigious transnational institutions as the United Nations and the European Union have endorsed censorship of hate speech, as well as denial of Holocaust and climate change, and even blasphemy.

Those trends are antithetical to classically liberal ideals about both the freedom of speech and the purpose of the university. John Stuart Mill thought higher education should not tell us what it is our duty to believe, but should "help us to form our own belief in a manner worthy of intelligent beings." He added that "there ought to exist the fullest liberty of professing and discussing, as a matter of ethical conviction, any doctrine," regardless of its falsity, immorality, or even harmfulness.

The classical liberal argument for free speech has historically been championed in two distinct ways. First, the Founding documents of the United States recognize freedom of speech as a natural right. Second, alternatively, that right might be grounded in utility, meaning its acceptance best promotes human flourishing. Ironically, the very trends on campus that threaten freedom of speech also lend strong support to both justifications for it.

"Freedom of Speech under Assault on Campus," by Daniel Jacobson, Cato Institute, August 30, 2016. Reprinted by permission.

Introduction

Many academics now consider freedom of speech just another American eccentricity, like guns and religion. What they call free speech fundamentalism is misguided at best, in their view, and an embarrassment before our more sophisticated European counterparts. Meanwhile, such prestigious transnational institutions as the United Nations and the European Union have endorsed censorship of a wide range of opinions classified as hate speech, as well as Holocaust and climate change denial, and even blasphemy—when called defamation of religion or incitement to religious hatred (and selectively applied). These developments coincide with the growing antagonism toward freedom of speech at American universities, especially from the most politically assertive groups on campus.

In considering this phenomenon, note that academia is now overwhelmingly dominated by progressives and other leftists, many of whom are not only skeptical of freedom of speech but intolerant of dissenting opinion.[1] When students protest speakers who challenge political orthodoxy, claiming to be oppressed by hateful opinions whose expression constitutes aggression against them, they often see no reason to limit their tactics to criticism and demonstration. Their violent rhetoric of aggression and assault encourages violent countermeasures. Not surprisingly, student protests are increasingly designed to punish their opponents and to prevent them from speaking or being heard: to shut them up or shout them down. The protesters are supported and encouraged by a vocal segment of activist faculty and are appeased by administrators—even when the protests shut down student events and transgress official university policy. Academic freedom, too, is now championed primarily as a matter of guild privilege, in defense of an activist pedagogy that promotes political orthodoxy and does not shrink from stifling dissent.

[…]

Speech and Violence

American universities have steeped themselves in the rhetoric of violence at the expense of their traditional mission: training students to form beliefs in a manner fit for intelligent beings. College campuses haven't actually become more violent. In fact, violent crime has decreased on campus, corresponding to its general decrease in recent decades. Certainly, Yale University—a recent flashpoint for the battle over free speech—is far safer than when I was a student there in the 1980s. Those days, the campus was less an oasis than a fort in the midst of blighted New Haven.[20] Of course, most campuses are far safer than Yale's. The current rash of violence is metaphorical, however, in that it fundamentally concerns opinions and their expression. This is a war of and about words.

The leading thought of this movement is that the expression of hateful ideas is literally an act of violence, which should be treated accordingly. In that view, words wound like weapons, and hate speech traumatizes its targets like the injuries caused by violent actions.[21] But according to the multiculturalist argument, only specifically protected groups of people are vulnerable to the harms of hate speech. (No one considers punishing a department head who calls Republicans stupid and encourages hatred of them, for instance, on the grounds that she thereby commits violence against conservative students.) Moreover, those of us who reject the assimilation of speech with violence, without engaging in hate speech ourselves, are often claimed to be complicit in the assault on victims of institutional oppression. Our arguments are not disputed so much as denigrated as vestiges of privilege, even though they protect the speech rights of all students and faculty regardless of their politics or identity.

One of the most blatant examples of persuasive definition can be found in the claim, now approaching a dogma in academia, that only the powerful can be racist. That definition is not the commonplace meaning of *racism* but a politically motivated redefinition, designed to obscure its subversion of the liberal commitment to equality under the law.[22] Even if the racially motivated murder of a member of a nonprotected group cannot be racist, because the murderer lacks social or institutional power, that does not change anything about the action's underlying nature. It just does not count as racist by stipulation, given the persuasively defined term.[23] But moral arguments cannot rest on semantic fiat. If the racially motivated murder of a "privileged" victim cannot be racism, because of the persuasive definition, that does not change its character. We could call it racist* instead, though that approach would be to capitulate to subversive semantics.

Perhaps the most objectionable aspect of such a rhetorical ploy is that it gets used to defend hateful and even racist (or racist*) speech against dissenters who are women or minorities—even when the objectionable speech is perpetrated by white men, so long as it supports the progressive orthodoxy. As a matter of sociological fact, the immunity to racism and hate speech ordinarily given to members of protected groups does not extend to those who fail to espouse progressive positions. On the contrary, they are attacked even more vehemently as race traitors, often in overtly racist or sexist terms. Women, minorities, or gays and lesbians who dare to stray from the opinions they are supposed to have—that is, those considered representative of their assigned identity—not only are subject to abuse by the supposedly oppressed campus activists but also forfeit the special protections they would otherwise be granted.[24] Thus, Ayaan Hirsi Ali and Condoleezza Rice have been disinvited and heckled at academic events, and they have been attacked by the very groups that claim to defend women of color against assaultive speech. But white progressive allies who champion the correct ideology—who "check their privilege"—are allowed to speak, albeit as social inferiors who must defer to their more authentic superiors.

In short, to advocate a position contrary to the orthodox ideology is de facto racist, regardless of the speaker's reasoning or motivation; but progressives are given broad immunity to engage in what would otherwise be considered hate speech against their political opponents regardless of race, class, and gender. Again, mere partisan intolerance of unpopular opinion gets framed as an exception for speech that somehow constitutes violence. Yet, such putatively hateful or violent speech is not identified by its motivation or effect, because analogous speech that targets dissenting opinion is immune. What matters is whether the speech serves the social justice ideology or not. That is the realization of Marcuse's "liberating" practice of intolerance, an overtly partisan goal carried out subversively.

In fact, the popular conflation of speech and violence is the inevitable consequence of the dogma that hateful speech is beyond the pale of free speech immunity. Here is the crux of the matter. The idea that opinions can *wound*, that they can *trigger* traumatic emotional episodes—which lead to (often violent) behavior for which the victim is not responsible—and that people should be *safe* from offensive views amounts to a substantive and dangerous claim that masquerades as innocuous and benign. The practical effect of banning hate speech is to present a new weapon to the antagonists of free speech: to argue that some doctrine is beyond the pale of toleration, one merely needs to claim that it constitutes hate speech. If putatively harmful or hateful speech is banned, then those who wish to suppress unorthodox opinion will attempt to frame it as hateful and violent. That is just what we now see playing out on campus.

Consider the degree to which political argument gets couched in terms that censure the motives of the opposition. We can put entirely to the side the question of the merits of various positions on gay rights. The relevant issue is semantic: positions held to be anti-gay are now almost universally called *homophobic*. That usage is highly tendentious, implying that the only basis for opposition to the legalization of same-sex marriage, or so-called bathroom equality, is the irrational fear of homosexuality. That is the nature of a phobia. The same rhetorical ploy is now being taken up by people who use the term *Islamophobia* as their analogue to anti-Semitism. Moreover, what can be done with fear can also be done with hate. When hatefulness becomes the criterion of speech that is beyond the pale, subject to either legal or social sanction, then that criterion creates a powerful incentive to label one's opponents' motives as hateful. It should be no surprise to see this happening.

The great irony of these developments is that they buttress both of the liberal arguments for freedom of speech, whether founded in natural rights or utility. The natural rights argument needed to show that the claim to a right of freedom of speech—properly understood, as the right to profess and discuss any opinion or sentiment, regardless of its truth or consequences—is better justified than any conflicting rights claim. The crucial point to notice is that the attempt to control the moral ecology of a campus (or the country) by banning putative hate speech amounts to just such a claim: that students (or citizens) have a right to a safe space free from opinions and sentiments that they find offensive. Note, too, that since it is impossible for everyone to be protected from ideas and emotions they find abhorrent, this right can be granted only unequally—to some, not to all. And no one proposes to grant the right to a safe space to dissenters. Thus, the claim of a right to a safe space free from hurtful opinions undermines not only the freedoms of conscience but also the principle of equality of rights. This point does not vindicate the natural rights argument for freedom of speech, but it shows that it rests on a much stronger foundation than does the illiberal counterargument.

The utilitarian argument for freedom of speech needed to show that attempts to promote the common good by circumventing individual rights would be so prone to abuse as to have worse consequences than a doctrine that tolerates all opinion and sentiment without exception. That argument gets even stronger support from the ongoing assault on unpopular speech in academia. The cognitive biases that undermine knowledge—conformism, group polarization, confirmation bias, and epistemic closure—are all exacerbated by the idea that certain opinions constitute "microaggressions" that should be prohibited and subject to sanction. A recent list of such heretical ideas approved by the

University of California warned professors against claiming, for example, that America is the land of opportunity, that the most qualified person should get the job, and that affirmative action is racist. By officially discouraging the profession and discussion of these ideas, the university shuns adverse discussion and undermines the mission of teaching its students how to form their beliefs in a manner worthy of intelligent beings. Instead, it establishes an orthodoxy of political opinion and encourages the punishment of dissenting opinion as racist or otherwise hateful and, hence, unworthy of counterargument. That orthodoxy makes political opposition tantamount to heresy.

What is more, such intolerance creates an incentive for hypersensitivity, since it empowers campus activists—again exclusively leftist activists—to suppress dissent. The multiculturalist assimilation of speech with violence, alongside the postmodern and progressive arguments that preceded it, amounts to an invitation to turn opposition into abhorrence and to exaggerate emotional trauma. This movement encourages the cultivation of intellectual vices that are antithetical to an intellectually diverse society by granting power to the thin-skinned and the hotheaded—or at any rate to those most ready to claim injury or to threaten violence. And it does so subversively, by pretending to enforce norms of civility and tolerance, while doing violence to the classically liberal ideals of a freethinking and intellectually diverse university.

Notes

1. See Daniel B. Klein and Charlotta Stern, "Groupthink in Academia: Majoritarian Departmental Politics and the Professional Pyramid." *The Independent Review* 13 (2009): 585-600. See also José L. Duarte, Jarret T. Crawford, Charlotta Stern, Jonathan Haidt, Lee Jussim, and Philip E. Tetlock, "Political Diversity Will Improve Social Psychological Science," *Behavioral and Brain Sciences* 38 (2015): 1-13.

2. This essay endorses norms of academic freedom and non-indoctrination, in line with not just the classically liberal approach but also common assumptions about the mission of academia (at least outside of religious institutions, which advertise their alternative missions), and to illustrate ways in which our universities are increasingly deviating from those norms. That is not to say that private universities must be legally required to adhere to free speech. If Harvard were to declare itself a Progressive institution dedicated to social justice, even at the

expense of academic freedom, then they should not be barred from doing so. That would be a bad idea, but—putting to the side complex issues about tax exemptions and the like—plenty of bad ideas should not be legally prohibited.

3. John Stuart Mill, "Inaugural Address Delivered to the University of St. Andrews," February 1, 1867, in *Collected Works,* 11 ed., John M. Robson (Toronto: University of Toronto Press, 1984), p. 248.

4. John Stuart Mill, "*On Liberty*" (1859), in *Collected Works* 18, ed. John M. Robson (Toronto: University of Toronto Press, 1984), p. 228fn. Mill's advocacy for tolerating opinions and sentiments regardless of claims about their "pernicious consequences" (ibid., p. 234) is often misconstrued by those who attribute to him a "harm principle" rather than what he more aptly termed a principle of liberty. For more discussion, see Daniel Jacobson, "Review of David O. Brink, *Mill's Progressive Principles,*" *Ethics* 126, no. 1 (2015): 204-10.

5. Friedrich Nietzsche, *Beyond Good and Evil*, trans. and ed. Walter Kaufmann (New York: Vintage, 1966), p. 90.

6. It is important to differentiate between legal rights, which are established procedurally, and moral rights that purport to be independent and prior to the law. Natural rights claims (like "human rights") are about moral rights.

7. The term *liberal* used to describe a coherent set of beliefs and values centered around liberty, which stressed individual rights and personal responsibility. Even in 1973, Milton Friedman described himself simply as a liberal, in *Capitalism and Freedom*, without fear of massive misunderstanding. But that semantic battle is lost; outside of a few circles, one now needs to refer to *classical* liberalism to refer to this position rather than generic progressivism.

8. Ironically, the metaphor was inapt from its conception, as the case that spawned the cliché, *Schenk v. United States*, concerned anti-war protesters in World War I who circulated pamphlets opposing the draft. Nevertheless, the point remains that the intentional provocation of a panic, when it constitutes a clear and present danger, is not protected speech under the First Amendment.

9. For just one example, see Robert C. Post, ed., *Censorship and Silencing: Practices of Cultural Regulation* (Los Angeles, CA: The Getty Research Institute, 1998), especially Post's introduction to the volume. Post is the dean and the Sol and Lillian Goldman Professor at Yale Law School; he is a constitutional law scholar who specializes in the First Amendment. The locus classicus for the postmodern argument is perhaps Stanley Fish, *There's No Such Thing as Free Speech…and It's a Good Thing, Too* (New York: Oxford University Press, 1994).

10. "We suppose the majority [of the poor] sufficiently intelligent to be aware that it is not to their advantage to weaken the security of property." John Stuart Mill, "Considerations on Representative Government," in *Collected Works*, 18, ed. John M. Robson (Toronto: University of Toronto Press, 1984), p. 442.

11. This account is not yet comprehensive enough to satisfy defenders of the free society—or even to reflect the state of First Amendment jurisprudence—but it will serve our focus on moral and political speech.

12. Secretary-General Ban Ki-moon, Press Conference at United Nations Headquarters, New York, September 19, 2012, http://www.un.org/press/en/2012/sgsm14518.doc.htm.

13. Quoted in Adam Liptak, "Hate Speech or Free Speech? What Much of the West Bans Is Protected in the U.S.," *New York Times*, June 11, 2008, http://www.nytimes.com/2008/06/11/world/americas/11iht-hate.4.13645369.html?_r=0. The exceptional nature of American speech rights is a longstanding theme of Schauer's work.

14. Post, *Censorship and Silencing*, p. 2.

15. Herbert Marcuse, "Repressive Tolerance," in Robert Paul Wolff, Barrington Moore Jr., and Herbert Marcuse, *A Critique of Pure Tolerance* (Boston, MA: Beacon Press, 1965), p. 81; emphasis added.

16. See *Michigan Capitol Confidential*, http://www.michigancapitolconfidential.com/17724.

17. See University of Michigan, http://publicaffairs.vpcomm.umich.edu/key-issues/guidelines-for-political-campaigns-and-ballot-initiatives/.

18. On this tendency, see Jason Kuznicki, "Attack of the Utility Monsters: The New Threats to Free Speech," Cato Institute Policy Analysis no. 652, November 16, 2009.

19. F. A. Hayek, *Law, Legislation, and Liberty* (London: Routledge, 1993), p. 243.

20. According to the *Yale Daily News*, "In 2008, Yale reported 296 major crimes on campus, one-fifth as many as reported in 1990. And New Haven has followed a similar trend—in 1994, there were 2,648 violent crimes in the city; in 2008, there were just 1,637." According to this article and official crime statistics, crime on Yale's campus peaked in 1990 at 1,439 major crimes and has continued to decline in New Haven since 2009. See http://yaledailynews.com/blog/2009/09/15/safety-in-new-haven-a-tale-of-two-cities/.

21. The locus classicus is Mari Matsuda et al., *Words That Wound: Critical Race Theory, Assaultive Speech, and the First Amendment* (Boulder, CO: Westview Press, 1993).

22. Although one might differentiate in an intellectually honest way between, say, racism and racial prejudice, those who make this argument typically trade illicitly on the claim that an action can't be racist unless it targets minorities.

23. This point is entirely independent of the issue of whether a racially motivated crime is as bad when committed by a member of a minority group as when committed by a nonminority.

24. Question: how can a Muslim student be subject to a hate crime that goes almost unpublicized on campus, and its perpetrators go unpunished? Answer: if he is a conservative or libertarian. See http://reason.com/blog/2014/12/15/social-justice-bandits-vandalize-apartme.

Liberal Academics Create an Environment Hostile to Conservative Viewpoints

Nancy Thorner and Bonnie O'Neil

Nancy Thorner is a conservative writer who has published essays in the Lake Forest Patch *and the Heartland Institute. Bonnie O'Neil is a professor of English at Mississippi State University.*

Obviously, Liberals have a very different philosophy than Conservatives. That is why a growing number of people are concerned about the unusual and disproportionate inequality that exists between Liberal professors and Conservative professors within America's colleges and universities today. When there is an inequality as great as nine liberal professors to one Conservative professor in a college, it is impossible to believe the students are receiving a fair and balanced education. Parents and the public are seeking answers as to why the imbalance exists and calling upon universities to examine how to create a more balanced environment and learning experience for their children.

Numerous questions are being discussed in the public arena, such as reasons for the severe inequality, and how it has or potentially might affect students and ultimately society in general. Parents are asking why they should pay outrageous sums of money for high tuition, only to discover their children are being indoctrinated by professors who criticize any and all of their conservative viewpoints, and thus create family controversies.

Parents state they expect colleges to teach facts and methods, but not specific philosophical ideals that are known to be controversial. Complaints are mounting that classes have become places for indoctrination to a specific liberal viewpoint, and conservative students are ridiculed for making any comments that disagree with the professors' opinions. Parents believe it is most important for

"Why Are Our Colleges and Universities Dominated by Liberals?" by Nancy Thorner and Bonnie O'Neil, The Heartland Institute, December 9, 2014. Reprinted by permission.

professors to explain both sides of controversial issues equally to give students the opportunity to discern for themselves what they believe. Success beyond college is often determined by more than just knowledge, but by students who have been given the advantage of hearing and knowing both sides of the political debate, and thus able to better understand others' opinions and their frame of reference, while comfortably committed to their own belief system.

In a provocative article, "Why Are So Many College Professors Politically Liberal," the author claims students seeking professorships are those whose views are already liberal in nature. Furthermore, professors who wish to indoctrinate, rather than educate, are not nearly as common as some people would indicate. That may be true, but evidence also indicates there is a definite bias in hiring practices by most universities, especially Ivy League schools.

The most unreasonable falsehood by liberals is to claim that modern conservatism is so shot through with anti-intellectualism that it should not be surprising when intellectuals (liberals) want nothing to do with conservatism and certainly aren't attracted to it. This narrow, rather supercilious viewpoint is witnessed in a liberal's response to Conservative thinker William F. Buckley, who was noted for representing the best of serious conservative thought. Liberals, rather than respect or provide information that factually contradicted Buckley's viewpoints, instead chose to personally attack Buckley's character rather than his ideas, in order to defend their liberal positions. They even had the audacity to claim Buckley's viewpoints were "preening, self-righteous, borderline bigoted nonsense."

The explanation presented by Chris Mooney in his article—"Yes, Liberals Rule the Ivory Tower—But Why?"—acclaims academia is more liberal than America because these are the individuals who prefer academia, just like other professions attract a larger proportion of conservatives, i.e., the clergy and the military. As to the reason: The ivory tower's well-known political reputation has encouraged a kind of self-selection effect. Conservatives gravitate away from it and liberals towards it. Thus, people who are godless and liberal tend to seek university and college positions and are comfortable there.

Dr. Wood, a political conservative and a former professor of anthropology and associate provost at Boston University, believes that the claim Conservatives are self-selecting other careers is but part of the story. It is the reason behind the self-selecting claim that is most important. Conservative know they will be shunned, ignored, minimized, and/or not able to advance. Dr. Wood made this logical statement that is hard to dispute:

> *The most effective way to keep out a whole class of people who are unwelcome isn't to bar entry, but to make sure that very few in that class will want to enter.*

Intolerance of Conservatives

It is not a secret within the halls of higher learning that Conservatives are generally not invited to the parties, not awarded grants, nor usually promoted within the university. Conservatives are left to wonder how they might respond to negative jokes about issues or people they respect. Obviously, it would be a difficult decision for a graduate student to apply for any job that places him in a daily uncomfortable position among his peers, who smugly brag about their disdain for conservative thought.

Should the public care whether Liberals discriminate against Conservatives and thus create a serious imbalance of political, social, and spiritual opinions in the classrooms? Yes, everyone, including liberals, should be very concerned about prejudice wherever it is found. Writing in the *Chronicle of Higher Education*, Dr. Wood criticized liberal social scientists for failing to heed their own extensive research into the harm of bias. They violate their own principles, blinded as they are to how bias has a negative impact on the students they teach and society in general.

A lack of political and religious diversity among college teachers robs students of passionate discussions from both a liberal and conservative perspective. Students who enter the workplace will be unprepared to understand the full extent of controversial issues which will confront them at some point. Students benefit from a diversity of thought, especially when presented by teachers who can passionately address the class with their own well-thought-out opinions. Diversity in professors, subjects, styles of teaching, and especially differences about controversial issues, tend to benefit students. It promotes creative thinking and provides an opportunity and advantage for the student to hear both viewpoints, thus helping them arrive at their own conclusion.

The question is not whether the imbalance should remain. It must not, because all schools should equally represent the diversity that exists within the public domain. The problem is how to correct the injustice of schools already dominated by liberals and liberal thought. Change is difficult, especially when those guilty of causing the imbalance are unwilling to give up the dominance they currently enjoy.

One question often asked is how did this highly liberal imbalance occur in the first place. Some claim it began with the debate and/or opposition to the Viet Nam War. That war became a catalyst for radicals to create chaos right here in America, and ended up with radicals bombing facilities in the United States, causing deaths. Some of those activists who failed in their revolt and thus goal to fundamentally change America ended up in our colleges. Their battle plan failed, but their zeal to reinvent America lived on. They went into the field of academia, where they waged a quieter war in classrooms by practicing indoctrination tactics on young, vulnerable students. Changing America's direction was much easier and more effective being a professor than a radical fighter who bombed American entities.

Examples of Former Left-Wing Radicals who Became Professors in America's Schools

Kathy Boudin was convicted in 1984 of felony murder for her participation in the Brink's robbery of 1981 which resulted in the killings of two police officers and a security guard. A law partner of Kathy Boudin's father arranged for a plea bargain. Boudin pled guilty to one count of felony murder and robbery in exchange for one 20-years to life sentence. Boudin's companion wasn't so lucky. David Gilbert received 70-years-to-life and is still incarcerated. With their jail sentence looming, the couple allowed their son to be adopted by William Ayers and his wife Bernardine Dohrn, both former terrorists who by this time were already respected university professors. Released from prison in 2003 (her partner is still in jail) Boudin landed a coveted teaching position at Columbia University. As a professor at Columbia in 2013, Boudin was named the 2013 Sheinberg Scholar-in-Residence at NYU Law School.

Perhaps the most famous example of a radical who became a professor is Bill Ayers. Ayers was a leader of the Weather Underground bombers in the 1960's. Bill Ayers (now retired from the University of Chicago) and his wife, Bernadine Dohrn (also a former Sheinberg Scholar-in-Residence at NYU), both became professors. Dohrn's tenure on the FBI's Most Wanted List never dented the confidence of the University of Illinois or Northwestern University to hire her. Ayers and Dohrn have long maintained that their bombing campaigns never deliberately targeted people. Ayers, Dohrn and Howard Machtniger, also a Weather Underground bomber, spent most of the 1970's "underground" attempting to avoid prosecution on a variety of charges, including a foiled attempt to bomb the Detroit Police Officers Association Building. Nevertheless, before retiring, Machtinger also became a professor at North Carolina Central University and Teaching Fellows Director of North Carolina, Chapel Hill's School of Education.

Former Black Panther party grandee, Ericka Huggins, although acquitted, was brought to trial on charges of "aiding and abetting" the murder of Alex Rackley, a fellow Panther they wrongly believed to be a police informant. Huggins later became a professor of women's studies at California State University and a professor of sociology at Laney and Berkley City College.

Susan Rosenberg a Weather Underground member, spent 16 years in prison for her involvement in the Brink's robbery.

Not long after Bill Clinton commuted her sentence, Rosenberg took a position teaching at John Jay College in the Criminal Justice Interdisciplinary Studies Program.

Another Weather Underground member, Eleanor Raskin, fled after being indicted for bomb making in the 1970's, but later the charge were dropped. Raskin became an associate professor at Albany Law School. Her husband, Mark Rudd, a Weather leader who fled and went underground, was eventually convicted in 1977, and sentenced to a two years' probation. Raskin later taught at Central New Mexico Community College.

Most readers will remember the lefty college professor, Ward Churchill. He's the former University of Colorado ethnic studies professor who claimed that the United States deserved the September 11, 2001 attacks because of "ongoing genocidal American imperialism." Although administrators at CU-Boulder concluded that Churchill's obscure 2001 essay, "On the Justice of Roosting Chickens," was protected under the First Amendment and the university would have to keep tenured professor Ward Churchill employed, Churchill was eventually fired in 2007 for (unrelated) plagiarism and fabricated research.

Fairness only a Pipe Dream?

As stated by Michael Moynihan in "How 1960's Radicals Ended Up Teaching Your Kids":

> So go ahead and commit a crime, "expropriate" a bank. Just make sure you leave an incoherent manifesto at the scene, claiming that you are shooting your guns and filling your pockets with loot "for the people," because when caught, you won't be a convicted murderer, but a "political prisoner." And when released, you too can be a college professor.

This isn't how it should be. The high cost of education has caused many students to end up with huge college-related debts. Shouldn't both parents and students be receiving the biggest bang for all the bucks they spend on higher education? Certainly all objective people can agree there needs to be more fairness in hiring practices for professors. We must begin demanding fairness in presenting students a fair version of all controversial issues. Parents and all citizens should demand our schools provide not only a quality education, but one that promotes equality as well.

How Can the Biased Liberal Agenda in Colleges be Curtailed and/or Stopped?

Public awareness is an important ingredient to stop the biased hiring practices. Facts are our friends, but the media tends to protect the liberal agenda and those who promote it. It will take concerned citizens everywhere to voice their strong objections before we can expect change to happen.

One recent story emerged that is both discouraging and encouraging. Before becoming a Professor at the University of Illinois, James Kilgore had been a member of the Symbionese Liberation Army in the 1970s. He spent five years in prison for his part in a bank robbery in which a victim was murdered. When the story emerged, the University fired him. However, the University Trustees found a way to rehire him. They determined individual campus units are free to hire adjunct, part time instructors. Thus we discover the lengths liberals will go to hire their own. However, the action of one man might be an answer to how the public can force colleges to rethink their policy of hiring extreme liberals, especially those with criminal pasts. The *Chicago Tribune* reports that at least one major donor plans to withdraw his $4.5 million in donations to the school, if Kilgore is allowed to teach. Hill, who has been a major donor to the school, explained that he "no longer wished to be associated with the University of Illinois after the board's decision to rehire a former radical and criminal, but would make the money available only if the university "does the right thing," and not rehire Kilgore.

Mr. Hills' statement is what we all must demand from our colleges and universities: "Do the right thing." Let's all hold liberals within our colleges to their alleged commitment to diversity, which they prefer to apply to every subject other than the diversity which allows Conservative political thought to be on an equal footing to their own.

When the people demand equality and fairness in universities' hiring practices, we can expect a positive change in the right direction. Certainly society deserves our graduates to be open minded, with a complete education that includes knowing both sides of each controversial issue.

Current Attitudes About Free Speech on Campus Conflict with the First Amendment Constitutional Protections

Candice Lanier

Candice Lanier is a writer at the Christian Coalition. She has covered topics related to politics, culture, and religion.

Florida Atlantic University (FAU) has adopted a new "Free Speech and Campus Civility" policy, which essentially disregards the First Amendment. Though initially the document espouses the benefits of free speech, it abruptly launches into an assault on the First Amendment rights of the FAU community. "What we do insist on, however, is that everyone in the FAU community behave and speak to and about one another in ways that are not racist, religiously intolerant or otherwise degrading to others," the document reads.

But, this is in direct opposition to the First Amendment. The university has banned speech that is clearly protected under the First Amendment. It is also protected under Florida's constitution.

As FIRE notes:

> This policy prohibits a great deal of constitutionally protected speech and expression. The ban on "religiously intolerant" speech has the potential to chill speech regarding the Israeli/Palestinian conflict, which has been a source of recent controversy at FAU. Heated debate on this and many other topics could quite easily lead, on either side, to claims of "religious intolerance."
>
> Similarly, the prohibition on any "racist" speech could be used to punish protected speech on controversial issues like immigration and affirmative action, opponents of which are often accused of racism. And the prohibition on "otherwise degrading" speech could apply to speech on virtually *any* topic that offends another person.

"As Erosion of Free Speech Continues 34% Feel First Amendment Guarantees Too Many Rights," by Candice Lanier, August 14, 2013. Reprinted by permission.

FAU has a bit of a history when it comes to stomping on First Amendment freedoms. In March, the administration tried to punish a student who expressed uneasiness with a professor's assignment which involved stomping on a piece of paper bearing the word "Jesus." The professor, non-tenured communications instructor Deandre Poole, was placed on administrative leave but now has his job back, although he has been assigned to teach online classes.

Unfortunately, FAU is not alone in its aversion to free speech. In a recent survey conducted by the Newseum Institute, 34% of Americans believe the First Amendment goes too far in the rights it guarantees. This represents an increase from last year and is also the largest single-year increase in the history of the State of the First Amendment national survey.

University policies, such as those at FAU, and the decline in Americans' regard for the First Amendment is a growing trend. This trend extends to social media.

Kirk Cameron ran into some problems with what appeared to be censorship, on the part of Facebook, when his upcoming faith-based movie, "Unstoppable," was blocked. Cameron made the announcement on his fan page that Facebook had blocked fans from posting any links to the website promoting his film because the content was labeled "abusive and unsafe."

"We have been officially shut down by Facebook and unable to get any response from them," Cameron communicated on his personal Facebook fan page. "Unstoppable" was made in partnership with Liberty University. Following Cameron's alerting more than 500,000 Facebook fans of his ordeal, the social networking site removed the block albeit without any explanation.

Facebook has been accused by those on the left and right of being overzealous in determining what content is acceptable. The social network has come under fire for removing pages and content published by advocacy groups and dissidents in other parts of the world in addition to pages promoting heterosexuality and pro-Israel content.

Jillian York, the director for international freedom of expression at the Electronic Frontier Foundation, has commented that, "there is at least a case to be made that the simplest course of action for a network like Facebook would be to only remove content when it is required to do so by law. But then what happens to the kind of content it just apologized for?"

It's as though Facebook has a problem with the *real* world. In the real world dissidents and unpopular opinions exist. The overly sensitive can choose the type of content they want to view while those who do not wish to live in a bubble are free to sift through a variety of uncensored content.

As Jean-Loup Richet, Harvard blogger, observes regarding Facebook's community standards: "Individual interpretation of proscribed content categories may lead to erring on the side of "protection" of users rather than protection of free speech." And, though it is well within Facebook's rights to regulate content as it sees fit, *Slate* magazine ponders the following:

> The question is not *can* Facebook censor speech, rather, but *should it?*
>
> For years, activists all over the world have complained of arbitrary takedowns of content and unfair application of Facebook's 'real name' policy. Along with breastfeeding moms are people like Moroccan atheist Kacem Ghazzali, whose Facebook pages promoting atheism in Arab countries were regularly removed. Before he rose to fame as the man behind the January 25 protests in Cairo, Wael Ghonim experienced a takedown of his famous "We Are All Khaled Said" page because he was using a pseudonym. And not a week goes by where, as director for international freedom of expression at the Electronic Frontier Foundation, I don't receive emails from individuals from the United States to Hong Kong telling me their account was deleted "for no good reason."

Frustration with what is perceived as Facebook's heavy handed treatment of conservatives has prompted the organization of a Facebook blackout, scheduled to take place on August 25:

We are organizing a nationwide "blackout" of Facebook to protest their arbitrary and capricious policies targeting conservatives with censoring and suspensions. We are asking for all conservatives to suspend (deactivate) their accounts for at least 24 hours on August 25th. If you are a business or promoting a page and have a FB advertising account, we are asking that you also suspend that for 24 hours. (Eastern Time: 8/25/13 at 2 a.m.–Central Time: 8/25/13 at 1 a.m.–Mountain Time: 8/25/13 at 12 a.m.–Pacific Time: 8/24/13 at 11 p.m.–for 24 hours)

As far as Twitter goes, the company has had a couple of international issues, one involving confidential account information handed over to French authorities. This was done to enable them to track down the authors of anti-Semitic tweets. This gesture was the culmination of a legal battle that started last year when the French Union of Jewish Students sued Twitter for allowing hate speech.

Then too, last year following a request by German authorities Twitter shut down the account of neo-Nazi group "*Better Hannover.*" The group was banned by the state for spreading nationalist socialist ideology. And, it was the first time Twitter withheld content by request of a specific country.

In the United States, threats to free speech run rampant from attempts to squelch criticism of Islam to institutions of higher learning thwarting freedom of expression. The First Amendment is in The Constitution for good reason and it is alarming how willing some are to relinquish precious liberties. Ken Paulson, First Amendment Center President and dean of the College of Mass Communication at Middle Tennessee State University, opines: "It's unsettling to see a third of Americans view the First Amendment as providing too much liberty." This underscores the need for more First Amendment education. If we truly understand the essential role of these freedoms in a democracy, we're more likely to protect them."

The Conservative Prescription for Action Against "Liberal" Universities Is Destructive and Unnecessarily Political

Nicole Hemmer

Nicole Hemmer is an assistant professor in presidential studies at the Miller Center of the University of Virginia. She is an expert on the history of American politics and media. She works in the Presidential Recordings program, focusing on the Nixon administration and its media relations. Her broader scholarship focuses on the history of conservatism and media.

I owa state Sen. Mark Chelgren wants to tweak the dossier that candidates submit when they apply to teaching jobs at the state's universities. In addition to a CV, sample syllabuses, and some writing samples, he'd like one other thing: their party registration.

"I'm under the understanding that right now they can hire people because of diversity," he told the *Des Moines Register*. And where are university faculty less diverse than party registration? That's the theory behind the proposed bill Chelgren has filed, which would institute a hiring freeze at state universities until the number of registered Republicans on faculty comes within 10 percent of the number of registered Democrats.

Bills proposed in state legislatures are easy fodder for outrage—some wacky proposals get introduced every year. But Chelgren—who, it should be noticed, claimed to hold a degree in business that turned out to be a certificate from a Sizzler steakhouse—is not an outlier. In North Carolina, a similar proposal was introduced and then tabled earlier this month. And at CPAC, the conclave for conservatives held in Washington last month, newly appointed

"Eternally frustrated by "liberal" universities, conservatives now want to tear them down," by Nicole Hemmer, Vox.com, and Vox Media, Inc., March 8, 2017. https://www.vox.com/the-big-idea/2017/3/7/14841292/liberal-universities-conservative-faculty-sizzler-pc. Reprinted by permission.

Education Secretary Betsy DeVos zeroed in on college faculty. She warned college students in the crowd to be wary of attempts to indoctrinate them: "The faculty, from adjunct professors to deans, tell you what to do, what to say, and more ominously, what to think."

Fear of a liberal university faculty has been a feature of modern conservatism for decades, woven into the very foundations of the modern conservative movement—although the attacks on universities have not always taken the form of legislation or calls for "ideological diversity." The adoption of the language of diversity and pluralism serves mainly as a new way to skewer the left using its own vocabulary.

But no matter how often conservatives call attention to the ideological imbalance in the professorate, they fail to affect the makeup of college faculties. Indeed, faculties are markedly more liberal today than they were when the fight began. But persuading sociology departments to hire more Republicans is not really the point. Instead, these attacks have turned into a tool for undermining higher education, part of a far more serious— and far less conservative—project of dismantling American universities altogether.

First Came the Red Scare, then a General Fear of Keynesians and New Deal Sympathizers

It began with the communists. (Almost everything about modern conservatism begins with the communists.) At the dawn of the cold war, the Red Scare snaked its way through American universities, targeting left-leaning professors who found that not even tenure could save them from political persecution. The scare turned conservatives and liberals alike into happy red-hunters, as administrators and professors entered a contest of patriotic one-upmanship: loyalty oaths, hearings, purges.

Ray Ginger, a historian at Harvard Business School, was forced to resign in 1954 when he refused to take the loyalty oath Harvard demanded of him and his wife. They had to leave their home; his wife, nine months pregnant at the time, was forced to give birth as a charity patient. The marriage soon fell apart, and alcoholism claimed Ginger's life at age 50. Rutgers fired two professors and allowed a third to resign after they refused to testify before the Senate red-hunt committee. No US university would hire them, and two were forced out of academia altogether.

The university scare more closely resembled the Red Scare in Hollywood than the one within the federal government. With the government, the fear was straightforward espionage: spies and blackmail and treason. With entertainment and education, it was the more nebulous fear of brainwashing, a worry that there was a softness in the American mind that could be exploited by nefarious filmmakers—and professors.

For conservatives, anxieties about communist professors co-existed with anxieties about liberal ones. Indeed, a significant part of the conservative theory of politics was that the slippery slope toward communism began with New Deal-style liberalism. In his 1951 book *God and Man at Yale*, written in the midst of the university scare, William F. Buckley Jr. had little to say about communists. He instead made the case that Yale University had become infested with liberal professors who, in promoting secularism and Keynesian economics, had torn the school from its traditionally Christian and capitalist roots.

As McCarthyism waned, Buckley's argument became more prevalent on the right. Thanks to growing affluence and the GI Bill, millions more students were entering America's colleges and universities. They were unlikely to become communists, but Keynesians? That was far easier to imagine.

In a 1963 piece for his "Ivory Tower" column in *National Review* (a regular feature on higher education—underscoring just how much the state of America's colleges worried the right), Russell Kirk dismissed concerns with communist professors. "People who think that the Academy is honeycombed with crypto-Communists are wide of the mark," he wrote. "At most, never more than 5 per cent of American college teachers were Communists." The real threat, Kirk maintained, came from liberal groupthink.

And how had the academy become so biased toward liberalism? Because administrators promoted liberals and demoted conservatives. That was the common conservative critique, anyway. William Rusher, publisher of *National Review*, laid out the plight of these conservative scholars: "They face many tribulations. Advancement comes hard. They are victimized by their departments." Passed over for funds to support their research, Rusher argued, these conservative professors became a "neglected generation of scholars."

The arguments that folks like Buckley and Kirk and Rusher were advancing in the 1950s and 1960s are nearly indistinguishable from those conservatives make today. But while the arguments have remained the same, something crucial has changed: the case for what to do about it.

The Conservative Diagnosis that Universities Are Liberal Hotbeds has Remained Consistent, but the Prescription for Action Has Changed

Conservatives are certainly correct in their central claim: In the professoriate at large, and particularly in the humanities, the number of liberals and leftists far outstrip the number of conservative. This varies by field (you will find conservatives in economics departments, business schools, and some sciences) and by school (Hillsdale College and Bob Jones University are hardly hotbeds of liberalism). But in general, the ivory tower indisputably tilts left. Whether this constitutes a problem that needs solving is open to debate, but even among those who feel it is a problem, solutions are hard to come by.

In *God and Man at Yale*, Buckley held that left-leaning faculty should be replaced by ones more in line with the university's more conservative traditions. The best guardians of those traditions, he argued, were not faculty or administrators but alumni, who should be given the power to determine the college's curriculum. They would do this through the power of the purse: withholding donations until the university administration became so desperate that they restructured the curriculum and changed up the faculty to meet alumni demands.

What's important here is not the mechanism for change— Buckley's alumni model was unworkable (it assumed Yale alumni all agreed with his goals and had more financial leverage than they did)—but the theory behind it. Buckley was opposed to Yale's liberal orthodoxies not because they were orthodoxies, but because they were liberal. He believed the university should be indoctrinating students; he just preferred they be indoctrinated in free-market capitalism and Christianity.

Over time, conservative efforts shifted from changing the liberal makeup of the university to building alternative institutions and safeguarding conservative students. Organizations like Young Americans for Freedom and the Intercollegiate Studies Institute became gathering spaces for young right-wingers, while a swath of new think tanks were erected for the purpose of getting conservative research and ideas into circulation. By the 1980s, anti-liberal student magazines like the *Dartmouth Review* served as feeders for Buckley's *National Review* and other conservative publications.

But what of the professors? They came under fire again in the 1990s and 2000s. Books like Allan Bloom's *Closing of the American Mind* and Dinesh D'Souza's *Illiberal Education* popularized the idea that professors infected their students with relativism, liberalism, and leftism, laying the intellectual groundwork for a new effort to limit the influence of liberal scholars.

But when those attacks came, they came wrapped in an entirely new logic and language: ideological diversity.

Marshaling Liberal Arguments about Viewpoint Diversity in Support of the Conservative Cause

Let's pause here for a second, because this is important. In the 1990s, there was a real shift in American culture and politics, centered on multiculturalism and the postmodernism. Multiculturalism held that diversity was a positive value, because people from different backgrounds brought with them different perspectives, and a wide range of perspectives was good for intellectual debate. Postmodernism, a more academic idea, held—at least in some of its guises—that truth was inaccessible, perhaps nonexistent, that everything might be relative, everything might be perspective.

Conservatives didn't like either one of these shifts. Social conservatives like Pat Buchanan and Bill Bennett saw multiculturalism as a thinly veiled attack on the West (read: white European culture). Likewise, the rejection of knowable truths was an affront to believers in a fixed moral universe based on shared values. Multiculturalism, postmodernism—these were anathema to their conservatism.

Except—multiculturalism was also incredibly useful. If diversity of perspectives was good, and if universities valued that diversity enough for it be a factor in hiring, then surely the paucity of conservative professors was a wrong to be remedied?

Enter the pro-diversity conservatives, who have taken the arguments of the left and turned them into tools to expand conservatives' presence in university faculty. The most visible early proponent of this approach was a former leftist, David Horowitz, who in 2003 founded the Campaign for Fairness and Inclusion in Higher Education (later renamed Students for Academic Freedom). The very name of the campaign suggested that Horowitz was committed to a pluralistic model of higher education dedicated to equity and balance.

The central project of Students for Academic Freedom was the Academic Bill of Rights. In its definition of academic freedom, the Academic Bill of Rights homed in immediately on "intellectual diversity." It never mentioned conservatism, but rather advocated protecting students from the imposition of "political, ideological, or religious orthodoxy." Given that Horowitz had widely criticized the "one-party classroom" and the liberal atmosphere of the academy, this equation of academic freedom with intellectual diversity amounted to a call to protect conservative professors and students.

That same framework could also be found in the 2009 book *The Politically Correct University*, published by the American

Enterprise Institute. It included a chapter laying out "the route to academic pluralism" and another that claimed "the academy's definition and practice of diversity is too narrow and limited," arguing instead "for a more inclusive definition of diversity that encompasses intellectual diversity."

In some rare cases, conservatives borrowed the language not just of diversity but of postmodernism. Horowitz asserted that the reason there needs to be more ideological diversity on campus is that "there are no 'correct' answers to controversial issues." This is a long way indeed from conservatives' traditional rejection of relativism. Indeed, one could fairly wonder whether there was anything conservative about it at all.

So conservatives found a new argument for hiring more conservative professors. What they had *not* found was a way to convince universities to actually hire them. And this is the perennial problem with conservative critiques of higher education, the reason they scurried away into think tanks or places like Hillsdale college: There doesn't appear to be any mechanism to *make* universities hire more conservative faculty members.

This is in sharp contrast to the right's power to shape precollege education. Through school boards and state legislatures, conservatives have had real impact on public school curricula around the nation. They have won wars over textbooks, standards, even Advanced Placement guidelines. But that power smacks into a wall when it comes to higher education, where traditions of academic freedom and shared governance between faculty and administrators create real limits to external meddling.

Which is why conservatives are so often left lobbing rhetorical bombs at universities, and why bills like those in Iowa and North Carolina usually wind up quietly tabled. There is no legislative fix for ideological imbalance in the classroom, nor any general agreement that it is a problem that *should* be fixed.

The most interesting work being done on the topic of liberal academic groupthink is at Heterodox Academy, directed by the NYU social psychologist Jonathan Haidt. The organization brings together scholars from across the country who are committed to promoting greater viewpoint diversity on campuses. But look through the list of solutions Haidt and his colleagues provide, and you won't find a single piece of legislation among them. Indeed, what you'll find reading lists, student government resolutions, college "heterodoxy" ratings—is aimed almost entirely at students, not at hiring committees.

If Liberal Arts Departments Won't Hire More Conservatives, Why Not Defund the Liberal Arts?

The right is still intent on undercutting what they see as the liberal political power of the university. But they're taking a different tack, pursuing their goals in more structural ways: weakening tenure, slashing budgets, upping teaching loads. It would be easy to dismiss this as simply a result of austerity programs, which have cut public services to the bone in states across America. But in states like Wisconsin and North Carolina, however, the cuts have been accompanied by rhetoric that makes the true goal clear: attacking curriculums and professors who seem too liberal, and weakening the overall power of the university.

Take North Carolina. Since Republicans took over the state government in the Tea Party wave of 2010, the state's universities have been under constant attack. Centers on the environment, voter engagement, and poverty studies have all been shuttered by the Board of Governors, which is appointed by the state legislature.

No sooner had Pat McCrory come into the governor's office in 2013 than he began making broadsides against the university, using stark economic measures to target liberal arts programs, like gender studies, with which he disagreed. His stated view was that university programs should be funded based on how many of their graduates get jobs.

Notably, the McCrory campaign was bankrolled by Art Pope, founder of the Pope Center for Higher Education (now the Martin Center), an organization dedicated to increasing the "diversity of ideas" taught on campus. As its policy director, Jay Schalin, explained in 2015, the crisis at the university stems from "the ideas that are being discussed and promoted": "multiculturalism, collectivism, left-wing post-modernism." He wants less Michel Foucault on campus, more Ayn Rand.

But bills calling for the banning of works by leftist historian Howard Zinn or hiring professors based on party registration haven't yet made it out of the proposal stage. What has? Steep funding cuts that have led to higher tuition, smaller faculties, and reduced access to higher education for low-income students.

That is the real threat to the professorate, and to the university more broadly. And as with the strategic conservative embrace of postmodernism, it also represents an erosion of a worldview that once understood the value of an advanced education beyond mere job preparation or vocational training. Unable to reverse the ivory tower's tilt, many on the right are willing to smash it altogether, another sign of the nihilism infecting the conservative project more broadly.

Conservatives Who Dislike Campus Culture Should Respond with Rational Arguments Rather than Provocations

Spencer Grady-Pawl

Spencer Grady-Pawl, formerly of the American Humanist Association, is a contributing writer for the Humanist.

During my college application process, I kept a chart that showed the average high and low temperatures in January at each of the schools I was considering. I figured if I got to pick where I lived for four years, it might as well be someplace warm. Not the criteria my guidance counselor would have recommended I base my decision off of, perhaps, but it was important to me.

A recent Gallup poll has raised the possibility that other more unorthodox considerations may soon be playing a role in the decision-making of college-bound students and their parents—specifically, partisan identity. In a survey soliciting opinions on higher education, Gallup found that a mere 33 percent of Republicans and those who lean in that direction have *a great deal* or *quite a lot* of confidence in colleges and universities. The number one justification for these attitudes, given by 32 percent of respondents, was that universities are "too liberal/political," which raises some interesting questions about the future of higher education in this country.

The first question is whether we'll see a decrease in the number of conservatives sending their kids to college. We can be fairly confident in saying that this is highly unlikely, especially given that in the survey, only 7 percent of Republicans and Republican-leaners cited the difficulty of finding employment as the reason for their lack of confidence in higher education. If both Democrats and Republicans largely accept that colleges and universities

"The Failures of Conservatism in Higher Education," by Spencer Grady-Pawl, The American Humanist Association, September 11, 2017. Reprinted by permission.

are important as career stepping stones, then how can those on the right reconcile their distrust of the system with their acknowledgment of its importance? They can, as many do, fight for "free speech" on college campuses, and against safe spaces and the "special snowflake" status that they seem to believe appears on the identification cards of students at liberal universities. Or they can seek out conservative schools. For the moment, their approach seems to be mostly the former—attempting to create change within the system, rather than seeking out or constructing a parallel system. To be sure, schools with conservative reputations do exist—George Mason, Hillsdale College, etc., but they are a clear minority in the world of higher education. The closest thing that conservatives currently have to a parallel system are religious schools (Bob Jones, Oral Roberts, Liberty, or BYU), but of course, many Republicans would find these schools a poor fit as well— one may worship the free market and object to trigger warnings without believing that physical contact between unmarried men and women should be forbidden à la Bob Jones University.

In addition, if conservatives were to take the "build a parallel system" approach, it would betray the very values they claim to support—unrestricted free speech and exposure to differing viewpoints more generally, and here specifically, opposition to the perceived politicization of higher education. Outraged by perceived censorship and partisanship on the part of the liberal elite in higher education, and the echo chambers they believe this creates, conservatives would look hypocritical forming their own insular institutions where they only had to listen to conservative ideas.

It would appear, then, that conservatives are left with little choice but to continue down their current path, railing against the "coddling" of students and bemoaning and criticizing the anemic conservative presence in academia. With this in mind, I have two suggestions for them.

The first, regarding their current practice of losing it every time a speaker is protested: stop. The idea that rejecting speakers or topics is close-minded has become increasingly untenable in an age of technology and publicly recorded positions. If I want to know what Milo Yiannopoulos thinks, I can read and listen to his commentary online, from Breitbart to screenshots of his old tweets. Then, if I protest him speaking at my school, it's not because I've heard he is offensive and don't want to risk being exposed to his ideas; it's because I have exposed myself to his ideas, found them to be beyond what can appropriately be considered academic discourse, and object to their being given a platform that presents them as such. The so-called "debate over free speech" isn't really that; rather, it is a debate over what constitutes an idea or legitimate intellectual inquiry, and what is simply trolling, hate speech, or conspiracy theory. Only the blindest of conservatives would believe it was "censorship" if a school refused to attach its legitimacy and reputation to speech that, far from contributing to any sort of discourse, simply boils down to racist (or sexist, or homophobic, or xenophobic) opinions.

Assuming that my advice is heeded, the last and best option remaining for conservatives is to compete with liberals in the free market they love so much. In higher education, this would be the market of ideas. Economics is a field that tends to feature more conservatives (at least fiscal ones). Clearly, it is possible for conservatives and their ideas to find success at the university level. Here's the other thing: it's not like a majority of the unemployed PhDs out there are Republicans. There are simply fewer conservatives competing for these jobs. Perhaps that's because they self-select out of what they view as a liberal field; perhaps it is because education tends to liberalize. Perhaps it is because, as Stephen Colbert once noted, reality has a well-known liberal bias. Regardless of the reason, if conservatives are truly concerned about a liberal lean in academia, they know what they must do to counteract it. If they're serious about their concerns and ideals, they will do it. And if they're not, they will continue to complain and cry censorship and take shots at snowflakes without making a serious effort to put conservative ideas and academics to the test against those on the liberal side.

CHAPTER 2

Should First Amendment Protections Extend to All Speech?

The First Amendment's Protections and Limitations

Lumen Learning

Lumen Learning's mission is to make learning opportunities available to all students, regardless of socioeconomic background, by using open educational resources (OER) to create well-designed and low-cost course materials that replace expensive textbooks.

The First Amendment (Amendment I) to the United States Constitution is part of the Bill of Rights and protects American civil liberties. The amendment prohibits the making of any law pertaining to an establishment of a federal or state religion, impeding the free exercise of religion, abridging the freedom of speech, infringing on the freedom of the press, interfering with the right to peaceably assemble, or prohibiting the petitioning for a governmental redress of grievances.

The First Amendment

The text of the First Amendment reads, "Congress shall make no law respecting an establishment of religion, or prohibiting the free exercise thereof; or abridging the freedom of speech, or of the press; or the right of the people peaceably to assemble, and to petition the Government for a redress of grievances."

Anti-war protests during World War I gave rise to several important free speech cases related to sedition and inciting violence. Clear and present danger was a doctrine adopted by the Supreme Court of the United States to determine under what circumstances limits can be placed on First Amendment freedoms of speech, press or assembly. Before the twentieth century, most free speech issues involved prior restraint. Starting in the early 1900s, the Supreme Court began to consider cases in which persons were punished after speaking or publishing.

In the 1919 case *Schenck v. United States* the Supreme Court held that an anti-war activist did not have a First Amendment right to speak out against the draft. The clear and present danger test was established by Justice Oliver Wendell Holmes, Jr. in the unanimous opinion for the case *Schenck v. United States*, concerning the ability of the government to regulate speech against the draft during World War I. Following *Schenck v. United States*, "clear and present danger" became both a public metaphor for First Amendment speech and a standard test in cases before the Court where a United States law limits a citizen's First Amendment rights; the law is deemed to be constitutional if it can be shown that the language it prohibits poses a "clear and present danger".

Incorporating the First Amendment
Originally, the First Amendment applied only to laws enacted by the Congress. However, starting with *Gitlow v. New York* (1925), the Supreme Court has applied the First Amendment to each state. This was done through the Due Process Clause of the Fourteenth Amendment. The Court has also recognized a series of exceptions to provisions protecting the freedom of speech.

Background to the First Amendment
Opposition to the ratification of the Constitution was partly based on the Constitution's lack of adequate guarantees for civil liberties. To provide such guarantees, the First Amendment, along with the rest of the Bill of Rights, was submitted to the states for ratification on September 25, 1789, and adopted on December 15, 1791.

Comparing the First Amendment to Other Rights Protection Instruments
Some provisions of the United States Bill of Rights have their roots in similar documents from England, France, and the Philippines. The English Bill of Rights, however, does not include many of the protections found in the First Amendment. For example, the

First Amendment guarantees freedom of speech to the general populace but the English Bill of Rights protected only free speech in Parliament. A French revolutionary document, the French Declaration of the Rights of Man and of the Citizen, passed just weeks before Congress proposed the Bill of Rights, contains certain guarantees that are similar to those in the First Amendment. Parts of the Constitution of the Philippines, written in 1987, contain identical wording to the First Amendment regarding speech and religion. Echoing Jefferson's famous phrase, all three constitutions, in the section on Principles, contain the sentence, "The separation of Church and State shall be inviolable."

Although the First Amendment does not explicitly set restrictions on freedom of speech, other declarations of rights occasionally do. For example, the European Convention on Human Rights permits restrictions "in the interests of national security, territorial integrity or public safety, for the prevention of disorder or crime, for the protection of health or morals, for the protection of the reputation or the rights of others, for preventing the disclosure of information received in confidence, or for maintaining the authority and impartiality of the judiciary. " Similarly, the Constitution of India allows "reasonable" restrictions upon free speech to serve "public order, security of State, decency or morality."

Lastly, the First Amendment was one of the first guarantees of religious freedom: neither the English Bill of Rights nor the French Declaration of the Rights of Man and of the Citizen contain a similar guarantee.

Freedom of Speech

Freedom of speech in the United States is protected by the First Amendment to the United States Constitution and by many state constitutions as well.

The freedom of speech is not absolute. The Supreme Court of the United States has recognized several categories of speech that are excluded, and it has recognized that governments may enact reasonable time, place, or manner restrictions on speech.

Criticism of the government and advocacy of unpopular ideas that people may find distasteful or against public policy are almost always permitted. There are exceptions to these general protections. Within these limited areas, other limitations on free speech balance rights to free speech and other rights, such as rights for authors and inventors over their works and discoveries (copyright and patent), protection from imminent or potential violence against particular persons (restrictions on fighting words), or the use of untruths to harm others (slander). Distinctions are often made between speech and other acts which may have symbolic significance. The freedom of speech is not absolute. The Supreme Court of the United States has recognized several categories of speech that are excluded, and it has recognized that governments may enact reasonable time, place, or manner restrictions on speech.

Despite the exceptions, the legal protections of the First Amendment are some of the broadest of any industrialized nation, and remain a critical, and occasionally controversial, component of American jurisprudence.

Incorporation of Freedom of Speech

Although the text of the Amendment prohibits only the United States Congress from enacting laws that abridge the freedom of speech, the Supreme Court used the incorporation doctrine in *Gitlow v. New York* (1925) to also prohibit state legislatures from enacting such laws.

Protected Speech

The following types of speech are protected:

1. Core political speech. Political speech is the most highly guarded form of speech because of its purely expressive nature and importance to a functional republic. Restrictions placed upon core political speech must weather strict scrutiny analysis or they will be struck down.

2. Commercial speech. Not wholly outside the protection of the First Amendment is speech motivated by profit, or commercial speech. Such speech still has expressive value although it is being uttered in a marketplace ordinarily regulated by the state.

3. Expressive speech. The Supreme Court has recently taken the view that freedom of expression by non-speech means is also protected under the First Amendment. In 1968 (*United States v. O'Brien*) the Supreme Court stated that regulating non-speech can justify limitations on speech.

Types of Free Speech Restrictions

The Supreme Court has recognized several different types of laws that restrict speech, and subjects each type of law to a different level of scrutiny.

1. Content-based restrictions. Restrictions that require examining the content of speech to be applied must pass strict scrutiny. Restrictions that apply to certain viewpoints but not others face the highest level of scrutiny, and are usually overturned, unless they fall into one of the court's special exceptions.

2. Time, place, or manner restrictions. Time, place, or manner restrictions must withstand intermediate scrutiny. Note that any regulations that would force speakers to change how or what they say do not fall into this category (so the government cannot restrict one medium even if it leaves open another).

3. Prior restraint. If the government tries to restrain speech before it is spoken, as opposed to punishing it afterwards, it must: clearly define what's illegal, cover the minimum speech necessary, make a quick decision, be backed up by a court, bear the burden of suing and proving the speech is illegal, and show that allowing the speech would "surely result in direct, immediate and irreparable damage to our Nation and its people."

Exceptions to Free Speech

Certain exceptions to free speech exist, usually when it can be justified that restricting free speech is necessary to protect others from harm. These restrictions are controversial, and have often been litigated at all levels of the United States judiciary. These restrictions can include the incitement to crime (such as falsely yelling "Fire! " in a crowded movie theater); fighting words (which are words that are likely to induce the listener to get in a fight); true threats; obscenity; child pornography; defamation; invasion of privacy; intentional infliction of emotional distress; or certain kinds of commercial, government, or student speech. Speech related to national security, military secrets, inventions, nuclear secrets or weapons may also be restricted.

The flag of the United States is sometimes symbolically burned, often in protest of the policies of the American government, both within the country and abroad. The United States Supreme Court in *Texas v. Johnson*, 491 U.S. 397 (1989), and reaffirmed in *United States v. Eichman*, 496 U.S. 310 (1990), has ruled that due to the First Amendment to the United States Constitution, it is unconstitutional for a government (whether federal, state, or municipality) to prohibit the desecration of a flag, due to its status as "symbolic speech." However, content-neutral restrictions may still be imposed to regulate the time, place, and manner of such expression.

Free Speech Rights Are Critical from a Legal and Civil Liberties Perspective

Anthony D. Romero

Anthony D. Romero is the executive director of the American Civil Liberties Union, the nation's premier defender of civil liberties.

For all people of good will—regardless of party affiliation, race, creed, or color—the events that took place this weekend in Charlottesville were sickening and deeply disturbing.

Several clear themes emerged for me this weekend. And while they are pretty obvious, I thought I would share them with the broader ACLU community, in an effort to give voice to what many of us are feeling and to spark a further discussion that will allow us to move together with greater hope and resolve through what are likely to be troubling days ahead.

While the events of this weekend—with white supremacists holding lit torches—frightened and outraged many Americans, we can never underestimate the impact of these images on African-Americans. That rally reflected this nation's history of slavery, racial violence, and terrorism, which has left an indelible mark on our democracy to this day. As employees, members, or supporters of an organization dedicated to racial justice, we are all affected. Many of us are even more directly affected because we and our family members are the direct targets of the white supremacists. I know that speech alone has consequences, hurtful and deep, and that's why I believe it's important to place the ACLU's representation of white supremacist demonstrators in Virginia in the broader context of the values and principles that have guided this organization for nearly a century.

First, the ACLU unequivocally rejects the ideology of white supremacists and we work actively with all our might to oppose that ideology in diverse communities across the country and to defend the right of all Americans to speak out against those views. By budget allocation, the national ACLU's top issue areas are ending mass incarceration, protecting LGBT rights, and safeguarding immigrants' rights, demonstrating our commitment to advancing equality and justice with communities that are often the targets of white supremacists' bigotry and hate.

The ACLU has represented or publicly supported Black Lives Matter activists in First Amendment matters at least five times in recent months. Our work against police agencies' surveillance of activists has been frequently in support of the Black Lives Matter movement and American-Muslim organizations and individuals. We've represented and taken public positions in support of anti-Trump protesters more than five times since the election and represented one of the Standing Rock protesters in a free speech case. The ACLU has also defended the free speech rights of African-American environmental activists in Alabama against a defamation lawsuit brought by the toxic waste-generating corporation they opposed. This is all in the past year alone.

We are not newcomers to this work. We've defended individuals targeted for their socialist, anarchist, and communist affiliations, for anti-war speech, and for civil rights activism throughout our history. We have repeatedly defended the free speech rights of day laborers against city ordinances—grounded in anti-Latino racism—that would have prohibited their expressing their availability for work. The ACLU was founded in 1920 when the attorney general of the United States carried out his "Palmer raids" to round up immigrants based on their "subversive" views. And we stood shoulder-to-shoulder with the emerging labor movement of the early 20th century. The First Amendment—freedom of speech, freedom of association, freedom of the press, and freedom of religion—has always been foundational for our organization.

Second, and more directly related to the events of this weekend, there are important reasons for our long history of defending freedom of speech—including speech we abhor. We fundamentally believe that our democracy will be better and stronger for engaging and hearing divergent views. Racism and bigotry will not be eradicated if we merely force them underground. Equality and justice will only be achieved if society looks such bigotry squarely in the eyes and renounces it. Not all speech is morally equivalent, but the airing of hateful speech allows people of good will to confront the implications of such speech and reject bigotry, discrimination and hate. This contestation of values can only happen if the exchange of ideas is out in the open.

There is another practical reason that we have defended the free speech rights of Nazis and the Ku Klux Klan. Today, as much as ever, the forces of white supremacy and the forces for equality and justice are locked in fierce battles, not only in Washington but in state houses and city councils around the country. Some government decision-makers are deeply opposed to the speech we support. We simply never want government to be in a position to favor or disfavor particular viewpoints. And the fact is, government officials—from the local to the national—are more apt to suppress the speech of individuals or groups who disagree with government positions. Many of the landmark First Amendment cases, such as *NAACP v. Claiborne Hardware* and *New York Times v. Sullivan*, have been fought by African-American civil rights activists. Preventing the government from controlling speech is absolutely necessary to the promotion of equality.

Third, the First Amendment cannot be used as sword or shield to justify or rationalize violence. Violence—even when accompanied by speech—does not garner the protection of the First Amendment. It is also true that the airing of ideas—no matter how repugnant or loathsome—does not necessarily lead to violence. The violence of this weekend was not caused by our defense of the First Amendment. The ACLU of Virginia went to court to insist that the First Amendment be applied neutrally and equally to all protesters. Reasonable members of our community might differ on whether we ought to have brought that case. But I believe that having divergent views within an organization dedicated to freedom of speech is a sign of strength not weakness. I also believe the ACLU of Virginia made the right call here. Some have argued that we should not be putting resources toward anything that could benefit the voices of white supremacy. But we cannot stand by silently as the government repudiates the principles we have fought for—and won—in the courts when it violates clearly established First Amendment rights.

Invoking the threat of violence cannot serve as the government's carte blanche to shut down protests. If that were the case, governments would almost always be able to shut down protests, even when the protesters themselves are peaceful, because others could exercise a heckler's veto through violence or the threat of violence. We must not give government officials a free pass to cite public safety as a reason to stifle protest. They have a responsibility to ensure the safety and security of all protesters and may make their case in court for reasonable time, place, or manner restrictions. That is what we sought in our lawsuit in Virginia.

The hard job for us now is to find concrete strategies for healing the divides that were laid bare this weekend. For the broader society, this would require that white supremacy, bigotry, and racism be confronted and rejected. Freedom of speech has to be valued and heralded as the cornerstone of our democratic society. Political leaders must shape the political discourse to underscore what binds us together as people, rather than exploit our differences. And government officials must neutrally apply the First Amendment and ensure the safety of all Americans when they take to the streets to exercise their constitutionally protected rights.

For our organization, we must remain focused and vigorous in our defense of civil liberties and civil rights in every community and in every context. Our 97-year history of defending the constitutional rights of all persons—even those we disagree with—is imbued with a belief that these rights are indeed indivisible, unalienable, and granted to each of us in our democracy. Our job is to turn those promises and aspirations into a reality for all people. And that work has never been more important than now.

Limitations on Free Speech in Academia Are Potentially Destructive

Robert Jensen

Robert William Jensen is professor of journalism at the University of Texas at Austin. He teaches graduate and undergraduate courses in media law, ethics, and politics.

Since September 11, I have been speaking freely in the United States, a nation whose institutions have many democratic features. My free speech, which has been harshly critical of the leaders of the United States and their policies, has been disseminated widely through print publications, web sites, email, radio, and television. Most of the exposure has been in the alternative media, but I also have appeared in a few mainstream channels as well. Extrapolating from the approximately 4,000 email messages, letters, and phone calls I received in the three months after September 11 as a result of this free speech, it is reasonable to assume that tens of thousands, if not hundreds of thousands, of people heard my ideas.

So, while it is true that as a political dissident I have no chance at the access to mainstream channels that "reputable" commentators can expect when they repeat the conventional wisdom, my voice did get amplified by the combination of: new technologies that are relatively open and have not been completely commercialized; a limited but active and committed alternative press; marginal openings in the commercial-corporate media for dissidents who have some claim to "credibility" and can provide the appearance of balance; and the ease with which foreign publications and web sites could pick up my work (I am aware of translations of my work after 9/11 into Spanish, Italian, Turkish, Polish, and Swahili). I have been writing in public as a journalist or scholar since my junior

"The American Political Paradox," by Robert Jensen, CounterPunch, October 12, 2002. Reprinted by permission.

year in high school, and in the last three months of 2001 my work may well have reached more people than the total of the preceding 27 years. This suggests a society that takes seriously the concept of free speech.

Yet after this experience, it has never seemed clearer to me that free speech is fragile and democracy is in danger of disappearing in the United States. This claim rests on two assertions:

1. Meaningful free speech is about more than the guarantee of a legal right to speak freely and the absence of governmental repression.

2. Meaningful democracy is about more than the existence of institutions that have democratic features.

To talk about the state of intellectual and political culture in the United States after September 11, I want to go back to the early 20th century and the life of one of my favorite radical Americans, Scott Nearing.

A Radically Good Life

Nearing contended that three principles guided his life as a teacher, writer, and political activist: the quest "to learn the truth, to teach the truth, and to help build the truth into the life of the community." Nearing began his teaching career in 1906 at the University of Pennsylvania's Wharton School, where he was a popular teacher, author of widely used economic textbooks, and well-known speaker on the lecture circuit. He was on his way to what looked like a successful academic career, if not for one problem. He took seriously those three principles, and from them he formulated a simple guide to action: "If there was exploitation and corruption in the society I should speak out against it."[1]

That's when the trouble started.

By 1915 Nearing had been fired by the Penn trustees. They gave no reason publicly, but there's little doubt that his socialist views and participation in the movement to end child labor played a role. Many faculty members, including some who disagreed sharply with his politics, rallied to his defense, but to no avail. Rumors of a demand made by legislators of the university's trustees—fire Nearing or lose a key appropriation—were never definitively proved but whatever the trustees' reasons, arguments about academic freedom made by faculty did not save Nearing's job. So Nearing moved on to the University of Toledo, a public university with a broader sense of its social mission. There he quickly became an integral part of the university and community—until 1917, when he was again fired, this time for his antiwar activity.

Nearing lost his job but not his voice, and he continued his writing and political activity, including an antiwar pamphlet titled, "The Great Madness: A Victory for American Plutocracy." That landed him in federal court, one of the hundreds of political dissidents tried in the World War I era under the draconian Espionage Act. Charged in 1918 with attempting to cause insubordination and mutiny and obstructing recruiting, Nearing went to trial in February 1919 expecting to be convicted and ready to go to prison; sentences of five or 10 years were common at the time. But he was determined to use his trial as a platform to explain his antiwar and socialist views, which he did with his usual clarity and bluntness (often, by his account, frustrating his own attorney's objections to inappropriate questions by prosecutors). His arguments from the witness stand apparently affected the jury; Nearing was found not guilty for writing the pamphlet, although the Rand School was convicted for publishing it and fined $3,000. The US Supreme Court upheld what Nearing called a "unique decision."[2]

Nearing remained a popular lecturer, filling halls as large as Madison Square Garden for solo lectures and debates with Clarence Darrow and other well-known political figures, until promoters would no longer book radical speakers. When shut out of lecture halls, Nearing moved to smaller venues, down to and including the living rooms of other radicals. He continued to write books and pamphlets, many based on his extensive travels around the world, focusing on both the corrupt nature of capitalism and imperialism, and the possibilities for a socialist future. In 1932 he turned his back on the modern economy and began a half-century of successful homesteading with his wife, Helen, first in Vermont and then in Maine.

After 1917 Nearing never held a university position and was blacklisted by mainstream publishers. But he continued his writing, speaking, and activism until he died at the age of 100 in 1983. He went to his grave unwavering in his commitment to his three principles and clear that his adherence to those principles had allowed him to live what he called simply "a good life."[3]

The Expansion of Free Speech and the Contraction of Democracy

In tell Nearing's story in short form here for comparison to the contemporary political landscape. It is vital to understand both the ways in which formal guarantees of freedom of speech and inquiry have expanded in this culture in the 20th century and, at the same time, the ways in which American democracy has atrophied. Since Nearing was fired and hauled into court, legal protections for freedom of expression have expanded and the culture's commitment to free speech has become more entrenched, which is all to the good. But at the same time, the United States today is a far less vibrant political culture than it was then. This is the paradox to come to terms with: How is it that as formal freedoms that allow democratic participation have expanded, the range and importance of debate and discussion that is essential to democracy has contracted? How is it that in the United States we have arguably the most expansive free speech rights in the industrial world and at the same time an incredibly degraded political culture? How did political freedom produce such a depoliticized culture?

First, the expansion of formal freedoms. On this front, the progress is clear. During World War I, Nearing was only one of about 2,000 people prosecuted under the Espionage act of 1917, which was amended with even harsher provisions in 1918 by what came to be known as the Sedition Act. Hundreds went to prison. The war-related suppression of expression also was merely one component of a wave of repression—which included not only prison terms but also harassment, deportation, and both state and private violence—that smashed the American labor movement and crushed radical politics. At that point in US history it is fair to say that freedom of speech literally did not exist. There was no guarantee of public use of public space (such as streets or parks) for expression, and criticism of the government was routinely punished. In one of the most famous, and outrageous, cases of Nearing's time, labor leader and Socialist Party candidate Eugene Debs was forced to run his fifth and final campaign for president from a federal prison cell after he was sentenced to 10 years under the Espionage Act. His crime was giving a speech which pointed out, among other things, that rich men start wars and poor men fight them.[4]

The struggle to expand the scope of freedom of expression progressed through the century, although not without setbacks. Similar harshly repressive reactions surfaced again after World War II in the 20th century's second major Red Scare. The Supreme Court upheld the criminalization of political discourse in what became known as the Communist conspiracy cases prosecuted under the Smith Act of 1940.[5] The law made it a crime to discuss the "duty, necessity, desirability, or propriety of overthrowing or destroying the government," an odd statute in a country created by a revolution against the legal government of that day. It was not until 1957 that the Supreme Court reversed the trend in those cases, overturning convictions under the Act.[6] The 1960s and '70s brought more cases that continued to make more tangible the promise of the First Amendment, including landmark decisions that made it virtually impossible for public officials to use civil libel law to punish sedition[7] and established that government could not punish incendiary speech unless it rose to the level of "incitement to imminent lawless action."[8]

This history leaves the people of the United States much more free to speak critically of government action. For example, since

September 11 many people critical of US foreign and military policy have written and spoken in ways that would have without question landed us in jail in previous eras. A sampling of the titles of pieces I wrote, alone and with my political colleague Rahul Mahajan, gives a flavor of the nature of our dissent: "Why I will not rally around the president," "US just as guilty of committing own violent acts," "War of lies," "Saying goodbye to patriotism."[9] In public speaking and in print, I have argued that the US war on terrorism is a disastrous policy that has more to do with the maintenance of imperial credibility and the extension of US dominance in Central Asia and the Middle East than battling terrorism. I have denounced patriotism as an intellectually and morally bankrupt concept.

I wrote all this as a faculty member of a public university in a politically conservative state. Although there was a letter-writing campaign aimed at getting me fired and I was publicly condemned as a "fountain of undiluted foolishness" by the president of my university, there has been no serious suggestion (that I know of) by anyone in the university that I should be fired. No law enforcement agents have knocked on my door. No judge or jury has passed judgment on me. While many readers who objected to my views have called for my firing, just as many of my critics have said they defend my right to speak even if they find what I say stupid or offensive. I have been called a lot of names, but no formal sanctions have been applied. And, more important, I have never seriously expected formal sanctions for these activities.

It is important to note here that I am white and American-born, with a "normal" sounding American name (meaning, one with European roots). The hostility toward some faculty members has not stayed within such civil boundaries, most notably Sami Al-Arian, the tenured Palestinian computer science professor at the University of South Florida who was vilified in the mass media and fired in December 2001 for his political views. It likely that not only my tenured status—I can't be fired without cause, protection that few people in this economy have—but my white skin helped protect me.

In short: I live in a society that is more tolerant of dissidents, legally and culturally, than the one in which Scott Nearing lived. For this, I am grateful. We must always remember that those expansions of our freedom to speak were not gifts from enlightened politicians and judges, but a legacy of the struggles of popular movements—socialists, labor leaders, civil-rights organizers, and antiwar demonstrators.[10] The freedom of speech we enjoy today was won by people who were despised and denigrated in their time. History has vindicated them, but in their own time they suffered greatly.

[...]

Notes

[1] Scott Nearing, The Making of a Radical: A Political Autobiography (White River Junction, Vermont: Chelsea Green Publishing, 2000), p. 56.

[2] Ibid., p. 117.

[3] Helen Nearing and Scott Nearing, Living the Good Life (New York: Schocken Books, 1970).

[4] Debs v. United States, 249 U.S. 211 (1919)

[5] Dennis v. United States, 341 U.S. 494 (1951).

[6] Yates v. United States, 354 U.S. 298 (1957).

[7] New York Times Co. v. Sullivan, 376 U.S. 254 (1964)

[8] Brandenburg v. Ohio, 395 U.S. 444 (1969).

[9] Available online at http://uts.cc.utexas.edu/~rjensen/freelance/freelance.htm or http://www.nowarcollective.com/analysis.htm.

[10] David Kairys, "Freedom of Speech," in Kairys, ed., The Politics of Law: A Progressive Critique, 3rd ed. (New York: Basic Books, 1998), pp. 190-215.

Some Hateful and Subversive Speech Threatens Civil Society

Traci Yoder

Traci Yoder is the director of research and education for the National Lawyers Guild.

During this time of controversy on campuses over the place of free speech within current political struggles, the role of the Federalist Society provides an example of how the conservative movement successfully legitimizes itself and spreads its message. Despite the conservative atmosphere of almost all law schools, and the current far-right influence in politics more generally, law student members of the Federalist Society still claim to feel silenced within the "liberal" context of their schools. Student groups and administrators invite far-right speakers under the banner of free speech, viewpoint diversity, and healthy debate, and portray challenges to or dissent against these speakers as attacks on the First Amendment (rather than seeing the protests themselves as protected forms of speech). While the Federalist Society does at least offer other perspectives by framing their events as debates, events sponsored by groups like YAF and College Republicans have increasingly been inviting provocative far right speakers the *New York Times* has described as "edgier, more in-your-face and sometimes even mean-spirited."

Competing perspectives on free speech across the spectrum of the left are worth examining at this fraught political moment. One popular approach, exemplified by our allies at the ACLU, argues that even hateful speech is constitutionally protected. From this perspective, speech that attacks individuals and groups based on race, gender, ethnicity, religion, or sexual orientation is both legal and defendable. The ACLU and many liberal-minded people assume that allowing all speech under any circumstances will ensure that

"Free Speech on Campus: A Critical Analysis," by Traci Yoder, Director of Research and Education, National Lawyers Guild, May 25, 2017. Reprinted by permission.

the best ideas win out and that it is ideal to have even potentially dangerous ideas out in the open where they can be challenged. They question attempts by universities to adopt codes and policies prohibiting hate speech, arguing that this well-intentioned response is incorrect and akin to censorship. Rather than restrict the right to use racist, sexist, transphobic, ableist, or other such speech on campuses, the ACLU recommends an educational approach that offers less intolerant viewpoints from which individuals can choose. A final important argument from this perspective points out that the limiting of speech on one end of the political spectrum can produce limitations on any speech found to be controversial, and will inevitably lead to greater restrictions on the other end.

This approach may seem logical and commonsense to many, and this line has certainly been taken up by the far right, who complain that the failure to include conservative views alongside liberal perspectives is a violation of free speech. On university campuses, reactionary student groups and their supporters draw on First Amendment arguments to promote agendas that are openly racist, sexist, homophobic, transphobic, xenophobic, and ableist. They claim that any resistance from the administration or the student body to these hateful ideologies is in violation of legally protected speech, and even ostensibly progressive universities have given in to this pressure by monitoring and censoring opposition. Extreme right fascist and white nationalist groups outside of universities also rely on the discourse of free speech to claim their views are valid and protected. While complaining about the "politically correct snowflakes" on the left, these far right speakers and their supporters actively cultivate their status as victims by attacking the vulnerable through their hateful speech and then claiming persecution when challenged.

From the commonsense liberal approach described above, the best way to address these kinds of speakers would be to let them express their views so others can decide if they agree or not. If all sides are debated openly, advocates of this perspective contend, the best one will obviously succeed. However, far right conservative and fascist ideology is not simply based on logical and reasonable arguments; rather, these movements depend on the irrational mobilization of hate, fear, and anger against some of the most marginalized and vulnerable populations. Offering them an open forum and vigorously defending their right to promote harmful speech confers legitimacy on their positions as being equally as acceptable as any other.

Another problem with the liberal free speech model is that is does not take into account the asymmetry of different positions and the reality of unequal power relations. Arguments about free speech rarely address the significant imbalances in power that exist between, for example, a wealthy white speaker with the backing of a multi-million dollar organization and members of the populations affected by their words (i.e. immigrants, people of color, queer and trans people, low-wage workers, etc.). What are lost in the abstract notion of free speech are the rights of those who do not have the connections or wealth to equally participate in public discourse. The "marketplace of ideas" is like any other marketplace; those with the most resources dominate.

Finally, the trend of students and local community members protesting reactionary speakers at universities has led to outcry about the "intolerant left" violating the free speech of the far right. But those who are so determined to protect the free speech of fascists, white supremacists, and other hate groups should be equally as concerned with protecting the right of dissidents to protest these viewpoints. While giving a speech attacking individuals and groups based on their race, sexuality, or immigration status is considered legal and acceptable by universities, the protests of those who find these viewpoints reprehensible are often censured or punished by the same institutions. It should give us pause that recent model legislation to protect "free speech" on campuses and to discipline those who protest controversial speakers comes from conservative think tanks The Heritage Foundation, The Goldwater Institute, and The Ethics and Public Policy Center.

[...]

Hate Speech Is Symptomatic of Toxic Underlying Social Dynamics That Can Lead to Violence

Elizabeth Dovell

Elizabeth Dovell is the advocacy coordinator for the American Jewish World Service (AJWS).

While hate speech can often be dismissed as bigoted ranting or merely painful words, it could also serve as an important warning sign for a much more severe consequence: genocide. Increasingly virulent hate speech is often a precursor to mass violence. World Policy Institute fellow Susan Benesch, along with Dr. Francis Deng, the United Nations Special Advisor on the Prevention of Genocide (OSAPG), is attempting to find methods for preventing or limiting such violence, by examining the effects of speech upon a population. Initiated in February 2010, Benesch's project, is funded by the MacArthur Foundation, the US Institute of Peace and the Fetzer Institute. It was inspired by the high levels of inflammatory speech preceding Rwandan genocide and the Bosnian war of the mid-1990s. Since then, the International Criminal Tribunal for Rwanda has recognized the relationship between hate speech and genocide by trying the world's first "incitement to genocide" cases, convicting radio broadcasters, a newspaper editor, and even a pop star for the crime. Following suit, the International Criminal Court has indicted a Kenyan radio host for broadcasts preceding the post-election violence of 2007-2008 in Kenya

In 1995 the ICC convicted Jean-Paul Akayesu, a former Rwandan bourgmestre—or mayor—for incitement to genocide after he gave a speech that was immediately followed by massacres. Benesch noted, however, that Akayesu's words did not catalyze

"Hate Speech Leads to Genocide," by Elizabeth Dovell, The article was originally published by World Policy Institute, November 11, 2010. Reprinted by permission.

genocide in the country, since mass killings had already begun elsewhere in Rwanda by the time he spoke.

Article 3(c) of the Convention on the Prevention and Punishment of the Crime of Genocide describes "direct and public incitement to commit genocide" as a punishable act, but does not describe the crime further, nor distinguish it from the broader category of hate speech. It is this existing law that Benesch strives to clarify through her project.

On October 28, 2010 Benesch joined Deng at the United Nations for a panel discussion on their project and genocide prevention. Populations do not rise up overnight to commit spontaneous, collective acts of genocide. Deng said. They "undergo collective social processes fueled by inflammatory speech."

One of the key points made during the discussion was the increasingly influential role of the Internet and text messages in transmitting and spreading hate speech. However, a balance must be found between prohibiting hate speech and encouraging the fundamental right to freedom of expression.

There is an important distinction between limiting speech and limiting its dangerousness, Benesch said. It is vital to examine the context in which speech is made in order to properly determine the motivation behind it—and the effect it is likely to have. The dangerousness of speech cannot be estimated outside the context in which it was made or disseminated, and its original message can become lost in translation.

Within context, speech can take on new meaning. "Are there particular aspects of the context that make a particular speech act more dangerous?" Benesch asked her audience on Thursday. "In other words, [are there factors] more likely to catalyze a particular form of incitement, like incitement to genocide, than other factors?"

Speech can also become less harmful if its sources are not credible, discredited or unseen by the population.

"The law has not yet distinguished fully between incitement to genocide on the one hand, and on the other hand the much broader and variously defined category of hate speech," Benesch said. She is working on developing a coherent definition so as to distinguish incitement to genocide from hate speech, a difficult task as a "particularly heinous crime is pressed up, conceptually speaking, against a particular cherished and fundamental right, which is the right of freedom of expression." The challenge lies in walking the fine line between monitoring and recognizing incitement to genocide and avoiding measures that may lead to over-restricted speech.

It is possible to limit the dissemination of speech if not the speech itself, which is a possibility that may be conducive to the goal of not infringing upon freedom of speech and expression. In striving to identify what it is exactly that makes a particular speech act "hate speech" on the one hand or dangerous "incitement to genocide" on the other, Benesch presented her theory: that hate speech can be performed successfully by anyone, but not everyone can successfully use speech to incite genocide. The power and influence of the figure addressing the speech to a particular audience, along with the contextual factors of that speaker and that audience (i.e. creating false scenarios of self-defense, in which the targeted group are accused of undue murderous acts), are substantial factors in distinguishing hate speech from incitement to genocide. The proposed policy responses include: logistical efforts to hinder inflammatory broadcasts (such as jamming radio waves), prosecution and arrests, and education. Getting the public involved and aware of the poisonous nature of inflammatory speech and how it can manipulate the masses is a key strategy in combating mass violence.

CHAPTER 3

Does Some Hate Speech Qualify as a Type of Violence?

Arguments For and Against the Criminalization of Hate Speech

Joyce Arthur and Peter Tatchell

Joyce Arthur is an activist, skeptic, and feminist writer from Canada. She campaigns for abortion rights and was a founding member of FIRST, a national feminist sex worker advocacy organization based in Vancouver. Peter Tatchell twice tried to perform a citizen's arrest on Zimbabwe's Robert Mugabe, getting badly beaten in the process. For more than three decades he has campaigned for human rights, democracy, global justice, and LGBTI freedom.

Should hate speech be a crime? Feminist Joyce Arthur and gay rights activist Peter Tatchell weigh up the pros and cons.

Joyce

A consensus exists in most Western democracies on the legitimacy of using laws to punish or inhibit hate speech, in order to prevent hate crimes, provide redress to victims, support vulnerable groups, protect human rights, and promote values of equality and respect.

Countries have international obligations to combat racism, which require enacting hate speech legislation. As in Canada, reasonable limits can be placed on freedom of expression to balance it against other fundamental rights, such as freedom from discrimination. Free speech is no sacred cow, anyway, since various restrictions are already accepted by society—for example, bans on threats, defamation, false advertising, noise around hospitals or schools.

While laws are only one tool among many to fight hate speech, they should at least be used against the most egregious cases. Courts and tribunals are capable of objectively weighing evidence and applying criteria to ensure that legitimate free speech or merely offensive speech are not captured.

Hate speech is dangerous because words have power and can influence others to act. The assassinations of abortion providers in the US prove that words do not have to incite violence explicitly to cause violence. Hate speech promotes division and intolerance; it harms and marginalizes the vulnerable groups it targets. Free speech is exercised largely by the privileged at the expense of the unprivileged who do not have a level ground on which to respond. Having no hate speech laws is unjust—as if people's dignity and human rights should be up for debate in the public square and 'may the best argument win'.

Peter

Hate speech is merely saying hateful things. It is not the same as discrimination, harassment, threats or violence—all of which are qualitatively worse and are rightly criminalized.

I don't approve of hate speech and believe it should be discouraged and challenged. However, I don't think it should be criminalized, unless it is expressed in a particularly aggressive, inflammatory or sustained manner, in which case it would amount to criminal threats or harassment.

One of the main problems with hate speech laws is defining what constitutes hate. Unlike incitement to violence, it is highly subjective. The line between hate speech and legitimate unpalatable viewpoints is hard to draw with certainty, clarity and consistency.

Several Christian and Muslim street preachers have been arrested in Britain for hate speech. Their crime? They said that homosexuality is immoral and that gay people will go to hell. I disagree with them but opposed their prosecution. What they were saying was hurtful but not hateful. They did not express their views in a bullying or menacing tone.

Free speech is one of the hallmarks of a democratic society. It should only be restricted in extreme, compelling circumstances. Criminalizing views that are objectionable and offensive is the slippery slope to censorship and to the closing down of open debate. It is also counter-productive. It risks making martyrs of people with bigoted opinions and deflects from the real solution to hate speech: education and rational debate. Hate speech should be protested and challenged, not criminalized.

Joyce

Hate speech is a public expression of discrimination against a vulnerable group (based on race, gender, sexual orientation, disability etc) and it is counter-productive not to criminalize it. A society that allows hate speech to go unpunished is one that tolerates discrimination and invites violence. Decades of hateful anti-abortion rhetoric in the US led to assassinations of providers, because hate speech is a precursor to violence.

Hate speech has no redeeming value, so we should never pretend it occupies a rightful spot in the marketplace of ideas, or has anything to do with 'rational debate'. Challenging hate speech through education and debate is not enough. Governments have a duty to protect citizens and reduce discrimination and violence by criminalizing hate speech.

Defining a crime with certainty, clarity and consistency is always a somewhat subjective exercise, but one that courts are expressly designed to do. Hate speech can be defined and prosecuted fairly without going down a slippery slope. An example is Canada's 'Taylor test' in which hate speech must express 'unusually strong and deep-felt emotions of detestation, calumny and vilification'.

Specific arrests or even prosecutions of hate speakers may not meet the test of criminal hate speech, and do not prove that hate speech laws are counter-productive. (In my view, however, only hate speakers with a wide audience or who engage in repeated ongoing hate speech should be prosecuted.) The justice system is a human institution and abuses can happen, but the answer is to refine and reform laws, not to scrap them.

Peter

I disagree that hate speech is an expression of discrimination. It's an expression of prejudice; not discrimination. Words and discrimination are two different things—unless the words explicitly incite unlawful discrimination; in which case they should be crimes because they incite criminal acts.

Mere hateful views shouldn't be criminal. Who decides what is hateful? The state should not have such power. It's open to abuse, as happened to anti-war protesters who abused British soldiers for their role in Iraq.

You suggest the police and courts are capable of distinguishing between hate speech and merely offensive speech. This is not true in Britain, where insults can be treated as hate speech. I was arrested for saying the homophobia and sexism of Islamist extremists is akin to the mentality of the Nazis. Separately, a youth was arrested for calling Scientology a dangerous cult. In both instances, it was deemed we had committed religious hate crimes.

Although it is claimed that hate speech influences people to commit hate violence, it's difficult to demonstrate that anyone has responded to hateful words with violent acts. The causal link is unproven. People don't kill abortion providers because they heard a hate speech. They commit these crimes because of a zealous belief that abortion is immoral.

I have some sympathy for your narrow definition of hate speech (the Taylor test) and that only repeated hate speech to a wide audience should be criminalized. Perhaps this is where we come close to common ground?

Joyce

In Canada, legal definitions of discrimination encompass hate speech.

I agree that people should not be arrested for the types of insults you describe. But one bad law or the abuse of laws is not an argument against hate speech laws. We are smart enough to craft better definitions of hate speech that protect marginalized groups from discrimination based only on immutable characteristics, which include religious affiliation but not specific religious beliefs or behaviours. Blasphemy must be permitted.

It can be very difficult to prove the causal effects of any law, but we accept living under a system of laws because they serve many other purposes. That said, a US court found that 'Wanted Posters' issued in the 1990s by anti-abortion groups for a dozen named abortion providers constituted a true threat because they led to the murders of several of them, even though the posters made no specific threats. People kill abortion providers not simply because they believe abortion is immoral, but because widespread hate speech against doctors creates an atmosphere of perceived acceptance and impunity for their actions.

Hate speech is destructive to society and to its victims. Enduring hatred over years can limit people's opportunities, isolate them socially, push them into poverty, lead to loss of self-esteem and depression, and endanger their health and safety. It is wrong to diminish the dignity and lives of some people just so others can freely spout hate against them. Leading purveyors of hate (at least) should be prosecuted.

Peter

I share your view that if a person is subjected to prolonged, extreme hatred it is damaging, wrong and should be criminalized. But this amounts to harassment and can be dealt with using anti-harassment laws, without the need for legislation against hate speech.

The abuse of abortion doctors is disgusting but I don't think it signals that it's okay to kill them. On the contrary, since murder is a criminal offence with severe penalties, society signals that killing doctors is impermissible. The 'Wanted' posters you describe were more than hate speech. They were *de facto* incitements to murder, which is rightly a crime.

We both agree that hate speech is a bad thing. We differ on how to tackle it. Hate speech laws address a problem after it has happened. I'd prefer to eradicate hate before it's expressed.

Suppressing hate speech by use of the criminal law is, at best, a short-term fix. A better solution is education against hateful ideas.

I'd like to see compulsory school lessons and exams in Equality & Diversity, to challenge all forms of prejudice, starting from Year 1 and continuing every school year. Production of the exam results should be compulsory for all job applications. This would, over time, debunk and diminish bigoted ideas; creating understanding, respect and community cohesion, without the need for hate speech legislation.

People aren't born hateful. They become hateful. Education can prevent hate. Prevention is better than punishment.

The Distinction Between Physical and Emotional Harm Is Arbitrary and Unhelpful

Aaron Moritz

Aaron Moritz is an independent researcher, blogger, podcaster, and video producer. His work covers a wide variety of scientific and philosophical issues, from sustainability and health to ethics and the nature of reality.

W ords hurt.

They don't physically damage our bodies, but the pain is palpable. It's also measurable in our brain activity. Social rejection activates the same parts of our brain as a punch to the face or a broken arm.

Test subjects at UCLA were asked to play a game of 'virtual frisbee', from which they were then excluded (after a few rounds nobody tossed the e-frisbee to them) and the pain centers in their brains lit up. The same thing happened when recently single New Yorkers were shown photographs of the partners who had left them—though we didn't really need science to tell us that breakups are painful, did we?

More to the point of this article, and just as obvious, is research that shows epithets and hate speech also hurt people. These words play integral parts in systems of oppression—subtly (or not so subtly) conveying contempt, hostility, dismissiveness, and rejection towards people in marginalized groups.

When I was in school, casually tossing around the phrase "that's gay" and calling people "f****t" was common. It stung every single time, even when it wasn't directed at me, because the message was clear: whatever was "gay" was inferior (or disgusting, shameful, unmasculine, etc).

Using the identity of homosexuals (and other marginalized groups) as a pejorative can sort of sneakily alter people's

"Words Can Never Hurt Me?" by Aaron Moritz, January 21, 2015. Reprinted by permission.

perceptions of us. This idea, called the Sapir-Whorf Hypothesis, says that "the structure of language affects the way its speakers conceptualize their worldview, and influences their cognitive processes." Homophobic language can quite literally rewire our brains to connect being gay with these ostensibly negative characteristics.

I know exactly what this feels like.

For me, growing up, being gay *was* disgusting (I was disgusting), being gay wasn't masculine (I wasn't masculine), being gay was inferior (I was inferior). That was, in large part, my reality. It took a fair amount of time, energy, and effort to overcome that programming—to the extent that I have.

Some people are never able to overcome it to any significant degree.

Thankfully, there is an increasing recognition of the way that power dynamics and oppressive positionality are reinforced by our language. This has led some to question the long-established logic of "freedom of speech." After all, if the language we use helps mold people's conceptions of themselves, is it really an individual "right" to use it in a way that dehumanizes disadvantaged groups?

Nancy C. Cornwell, PhD, at Montana State University, puts it this way:

> The individual, not social relations between individuals, is central to the classic liberal interpretation of free speech. This does not acknowledge that meaning is made in the relationship, not in the "relator" or the "relatee." Between males and females, blacks and whites, homosexuals and heterosexuals, the dominant group becomes the standard by which the "other" is defined. This power to define the "other" is the power to control meaning. Speech is not an individual experience, a right that is held at the level of individuals. Speech is meaning-making. It defines. It labels. It differentiates power. It constitutes the relationship between individuals. It is power. [1]

The entire article is worth reading; it's a thoughtful critique of traditional conceptions of free speech. I'll get back to free speech at the end, but the point that meaning is made in relationships and defined socially, not only by individuals, is a vital one.

Back in school, many of the people who said "that's gay" to express distaste did not intend to oppress or harm me. Some of them were, and still are, my friends. They didn't know I was gay, and had not, in their early to mid teens, thought through the potential effects of their words. Regardless, due to the homophobic culture we were steeped in, the troublesome implications and derogatory meanings *were* there and *did* affect me—even if they didn't always exist in the minds of the people who spoke the words.

This ignorance of how words can structure harmful (and seemingly inescapable) cages of context is extremely problematic, and should be fought by any freedom-minded person. Eliminating this ignorance empowers us to interact with these structures thoughtfully, in ways that encourage equality, human flourishing, and self-actualization.

We need to openly and forcefully challenge hate speech.

The battle has many fronts: in schools, online, at social gatherings, and in general public discourse. Each unique situation calls for a unique strategy—from respectful and calm conversation, to angry and forceful shaming, and everywhere in between.

This challenging of hate speech in order to reduce harm interferes at the level of the "senders"—those who, consciously or unconsciously, participate in perpetuating hate speech. We can also interfere with oppressive linguistic structures at the level of "receivers"—the targets, the affected, the oppressed—a sometimes under-appreciated reality.

We Are Not At Their Mercy

In the text quoted above, Nancy Cornwall seems to place the power to define meaning firmly and solely in the hands of the dominant groups.

This makes sense, because wherever deep, systemic power differences exist (and have been unconsciously accepted), this is the default. However, this dynamic is not like physics and can be disrupted.

As people in non-dominant groups, we can alter the meaning of these interactions individually, for ourselves, in any particular moment. We have the power to shift the conversation, and shift the meaning of these interactions to something that affirms our inherent strength, worthiness, and equality. We have the ability to exercise control over our own experience, regardless of what others are doing.

Meaning is not inherent, it is subjective, and we all have influence over our own subjective milieu. Through various introspective techniques, we can increase this influence—we can strengthen our impulse control, critical thinking, and emotional regulation—all of which sap away the painful power hate speech and epithets. Having support helps. Pushing for progress helps. Knowing, expressing, and building our strengths (with ruthless self-love) helps.

As individuals and as a community we can learn, and are learning, these skills. These tools are so powerful and transformative that I believe we have a responsibility to do so, and to teach others how to as well. In this arena—that of consciously altering our reactions and perceptions—we hold all of the cards.

They cannot dehumanize us without our participation. We are not at the mercy of bigots.

This is not to say I was "at fault" for the pain I experienced at school, but it does mean I could have done more to assuage it. I participated in it, because I had not discovered the tools to do otherwise. It makes no more sense to blame me for my reactions than it would to blame a non-swimmer pushed into the ocean for nearly drowning. The person in the wrong is the one who did the pushing.

But that doesn't mean it's not a good idea to learn how to swim.

Learning to shift my initial gut reaction to casual homophobia away from a reinforcement of my own inferiority, and towards a sign of ignorance (or pitiable malevolence) on the part of the speaker has helped me immensely. The word "f****t" doesn't have the same sting it once did, because I simply no longer believe the hateful implications it holds.

It could be argued that it is not our job to change how we react to oppressive language. Again, they are the ones in the wrong. We do not need to change, they do. They are the oppressors. This reasoning is valid and true, but I encourage us not to dogmatically follow it through to paralysis.

Becoming unshakably comfortable in our identities is not a luxury we must beg from others, it is our right and it is ours for the taking.

I refuse to release the reins of my emotional security to homophobes. It hasn't been an easy process, and I've nowhere near completed it yet, but I have proved to myself that I have a strong influence over how I react to and perceive hate speech.

I wasn't able to do this alone. Despite an often still homophobic culture, I have been lucky to live in a time with access to positive, self-assured gay role models who have fought for and won massive gains in gay rights. I don't know if I could have done what I have without that support.

Also, I acknowledge that as a white, cisgendered male, I was and am still enjoying the benefit of massive social privilege that has made this process easier for me than it will be for others. Some people will need more support than I did, and others will need less.

Nevertheless, I believe that we *can* each take care of ourselves, but that we need each-other's help, and that is not a contradiction.

Intentional Dilution and Unintended Effects

Our culture is becoming less accepting of xenophobic beliefs.

As this happens, slurs are starting to become more common with people who don't consciously hold homophobic, sexist, transphobic, ableist, or racist beliefs. Their *intent*, they point out, is not oppression. Often, they are used as an attempt at comedic irony, or due to a sincerely held belief that discrimination is no longer a problem, and the words are just ... words.

The question of whether (and how much) intent matters is controversial, and it should be. In most cases we have no recourse to knowing the intent of the speaker, and even when we do, it usually doesn't matter—it still hurts and still contributes to marginalization.

Nevertheless, I find it difficult to issue a blanket condemnation. Though the ignorant repetition of epithets by my schoolmates was hurtful, ironic representations of hate speech I encountered in popular culture often lent me comfort when I needed it most.

Shows like *South Park*, which caught flack from GLAAD for their episode about the word "f****t," were a breath of fresh air. For me, they took that word and disempowered it, using it to intentionally subvert homophobic ends.

It was like they took the bullet out of the gun.

This lived experience is not shared by every person in oppressed groups, but it was mine, and I don't see the value in denying its potency. These forms of expression had an extremely positive effect on my life and how I perceived my identity, and I feel protective of them because of it.

I am far from alone in finding solace, comfort, and empowerment in these kinds of self-aware comedic takes on hate speech and it is important to recognize and honor the vast potential for benefit they can provide.

Ultimately, however, I can only argue that they exist in a moral grey area. Some people have been deeply hurt by the same sorts of expressions that have been so positive in my own life, and we can't legitimately diminish their experience any more than we can mine.

That said, I think their net result is a contribution to making the world a less hateful place. When people use the word "f****t" in the context of *unambiguously holding no ill will towards gay people,* regardless of whether they are gay or not themselves, they are shifting the demographics of people who use the slur away from homophobes.

I like to call this process "intentional dilution." The more people use epithets without hate in their hearts, I believe, the more their power is diluted and stripped from those who would wield them as weapons.

I put all usage of hateful language without malicious intent into this category, including efforts by oppressed groups to "reclaim" epithets—the LGBT community's reclamation of the word "queer" is one of the best examples of this. These efforts too, though not quite as often, can have unintended painful side effects.

By reserving the use of certain words for only malevolent purposes, we place a loaded weapon in the hands of bigots. We imbue them (the words and the bigots) with more power than they deserve. We also run the risk, in our own communities, of shutting down intellectual engagement in favor of rote rules of acceptable language, and engaging in reactionary rather than thoughtful critique.

We deny ourselves the potential to recognize and appreciate complexity.

However, and let me be clear, I also believe (and this, too, is not a contradiction) that it is a *good thing* that activists criticize these same people I just defended. As I pointed out, the effects of what they are doing are complex and varied. This issue is not black and white, and the hurtful aspects deserve public and forceful criticism.

This criticism tells other oppressed people they are not alone, and that justice is being fought for. Having these conversations is an important part of the process of healing these wounds.

Even when intent *is* malevolent, the effects of hate speech are still complex.

The Westboro Baptist Church is one of the most hideous crystallizations of anti-gay bigotry in the modern west, and yet

I firmly believe that they have (unintentionally) done a lot of good for gay rights. They have illuminated fanatical Christian homophobia and made it explicit—creating the opportunity for direct refutation and mockery. They have become a standard of comparison for all anti-gay bigots, and this hasn't turned out well for the bigots.

Without their viciousness, the gay rights movement would have lost an incredibly useful tool—posterfolks for bigotry that can be pilloried and refuted.

Of course, that isn't to say that the Westboro baptist church hasn't caused harm. Of course they have, and of course they should be condemned for it. Protesting the funerals of soldiers and gay children is beyond malicious.

I'm not saying that what they have done is defensible, what I am saying is that we can, and have, turned some of their lemons into lemonade.

Finally, Free Speech

Throughout this article, I've attempted to demonstrate the complexity inherent in the meaning, intentions, effects, and perceptions of hate speech. Identical speech can empower one person, and hurt another, and speech that is nearly universally hurtful can have unintended positive effects.

What kinds of restrictions on free speech could possibly make sense of and take into account all of these factors? How can we determine intent? How much should it matter? How do we define which words, phrases, or ideas qualify as harmful? What kinds of effects would need to be demonstrated? It's not an easy knot to untie, and I question whether we should even want to untie it.

Harm reduction is a noble goal, but despite the real pain hate speech can cause, and despite the realities of oppression, I don't think that regulating the mouths of autonomous individuals is a good idea.

Actually, I think that it is really important to protect the legal right of hate speechers to speak, in almost all instances. I want to know, and I want society to know, what these people are thinking. Their ideas should not be suppressed, but publicly addressed.

Freedom to speak words and express viewpoints that were viewed as blatantly harmful, immoral, and disruptive was necessary in the initial stages of all social justice movements. We cannot lose perspective, now that we are beginning to win battles, and cut off the legs that brought us here. Gay author Jonathan Rauch puts it this way:

> Free speech is not only minority's best friend, in some ways it is our only reliable friend. If we can't speak in a majority culture, if we lose our voice, it is so easy to oppress us. The way minorities get real rights and real freedom is by fighting hate and bigotry and that's grounded almost uniformly in ignorance and fear. And if we're forced underground, if we can't show who we are, if we can't make our arguments, we are literally helpless. This is why I believe that hate speech laws are not our friend. [2]

Suggesting, even demanding, less hurtful ways of speaking is noble and beneficial, but any attempt to police the speech of others with physical force or law is a fundamental breach of autonomy and should be ardently opposed.

The precedent this would set inherently undermines the good intentions behind the rule and invites corruption. It designs and sharpens a weapon that has a high likelihood of being turned against us, and that I don't think we can rightfully use against anyone else, either.

This is not to say that any particular individual or group is obliged to listen to, or provide a platform for hate speech. It is well within the right, and as Nancy Cornwall argues (and I agree) the prerogative of teachers to limit hate speech in classrooms. The owners and operators of public platforms like Facebook, Reddit, or even physical auditoriums may decide to disallow any kind of speech they choose, though I would argue for a strong bias towards more openness.

We should not compromise our commitment to defending the speech and the words of people with whom we disagree, and should we ever find ourselves with the need to speak words or ideas that are denounced as harmful by others, we will be grateful we didn't.

Hate speech should not be banned, but those serious about liberty should make damn sure that it does not go unchallenged, or define the reality of our public sphere.

> If we don't believe in freedom of expression for people we despise, we don't believe in it at all.

-Noam Chomsky

Notes

1. Rethinking Free Expression in the Feminist Classroom: The Problem of Hate Speech—http://www.jstor.org/discover/10.2307/40545815—edited for brevity

2. "Knowledge starts as offendedness"—Jonathan Rauch interview

Free Speech Restrictions Reflect a Stronger Understanding of Free Speech's Historical Dangers

Barrett Holmes Pitner

Barrett Holmes Pitner is a writer and journalist focused on issues of race, culture, and politics.

The video of Sigma Alpha Epsilon fraternity members at Oklahoma University chanting "n****rs" would hang from a tree before ever joining their fraternity has sparked another furious national discussion over the limitations of free speech and the appropriate punishments for those who employ hate speech or dangerous speech.

And once again, too much of the media is focusing attention on the use of the "n-word" and not on the speech itself: a dangerous incantation and incitement to racial segregation, oppression and murder.

Last week's *Morning Joe* on MSNBC was another example of this absurd theater of moral equivalences. The show's hosts—Joe Scarborough, Mika Brzezinski along with conservative guest Bill Kristol once again attempted to explain to Americans that the problem with racism in America is that black rappers are indirectly brainwashing white youths to use the n-word. They argued that if black Americans do not want white Americans to continue referring to black Americans as n****rs, then black Americans should stop allowing artists and record companies to use it.

Essentially, the onus is on black Americans to prevent white Americans from using inflammatory, insulting language that has been used to oppress and demean black Americans since the beginning of the cross Atlantic slave trade. Unfortunately, there does not appear to be a social awareness or obligation to minimize

"Dangerous Speech is Not Free Speech or Even Hate Speech," by Barrett Holmes Pitner, March 18, 2015. Reprinted by permission.

hate or dangerous speech in American society concerning this discussion.

Regardless of how repugnant we all may find the n-word to be, it should be clear to any rational person that this scandal isn't about a black person saying "my n***a" in a rap lyric or even about a white youth saying it to his friends. This is about a group of youths gregariously chanting that those "n****rs" should be hanging from trees. One usage expresses the support of murder, and one does not. This is how free speech transitions to hate speech and then to dangerous speech.

America needs to start a debate between free, hate and dangerous speech. Internationally this discussion has progressed further than here. In America the emphasis has been on hate crimes, which advocates for increased punishment for crimes perpetrated because of hatred of another's race, religion or sexual orientation. Internationally the focus has shifted towards dangerous speech, which is a form of hate speech that clearly correlates to negative outcomes.

Susan Benesch, the Director of the Dangerous Speech Project in her paper, "Countering Dangerous Speech: New Ideas for Genocide Prevention," says that "by teaching people to view other human beings as less than human, and as mortal threats, thought leaders can make atrocities seem acceptable—and even necessary, as a form of collective self-defense."

The international emphasis of this discussion is centered around recent genocides and mass killings such as in Rwanda, Srebrenica and during the Holocaust; when the leaders of these atrocities publicized dangerous hate speech to disseminate ideologies of hatred to spur their followers to act, cow bystanders into passivity, and justify their crimes.

The hate speech used in these countries directly correlated to the commission of atrocities, and this discussion of dangerous speech could be beneficial in the United States. As a nation, America has tried to progress from the horrors of slavery, Jim Crow, lynchings and racial inequality while maintaining noble principles of free speech. Even now, the rather tepid addition of hate crime legislation constantly meets with resistance from many conservative lawmakers and parts of society. They argue a crime is a crime no matter its motives, and justice must be evenly meted by law enforcement. Coincidentally, the Department of Justice has just published its report finding that the Ferguson police department—and one would imagine many others in the country—is dangerously biased in its policing and treatment of its black citizens. It makes one wonder if any of the cops charged with protecting black communities were ever members of an organization or community that was comfortable referring to black Americans as n****rs? The fraternity scandal demonstrates how racist, oppressive and dangerous traditions are still alive and well, and may contribute to the continued oppression of minorities.

As a society we must become more aware of the dangers that certain speech presents, and for the safety and well being of black Americans and other vulnerable citizens, we must explore more robust ways for distinguishing and punishing people for dangerous speech.

Oklahoma University appears to agree with this position since they have expelled two of the students leading the inflammatory recital, and banned that chapter of SAE from the campus.

However, the two expelled students and the remainder of the defunct chapter have now hired high-profile lawyer Stephen Jones and are considering legal action against Oklahoma University and its president David Boren over their "harsh" punishment and "tarnished" reputations.

They argue that they are being unfairly labeled as racists and bigots, and that they do not deserve being "tarred and feathered"—an interesting choice of words; especially, since the two students have since apologized for their actions through a letter prepared by their lawyer blaming intoxication for their actions. When has intoxication ever been an adequate excuse for abhorrent actions?

These young perpetrators should feel lucky that they're not in jail. But the discussion in America has not progressed to a point where it sees dangerous speech—particularly racist incitement to violence—as a crime. The plaintiffs, along with too many Americans, are arguing that these "kids'" reputations have been unfairly tarnished. These arguments are either failing or not wanting to see the clear and present danger in their speech to black Americans.

Countries throughout Europe have seen the danger in certain hate speech and have created laws that punish racist incitement without compromising their democratic values on free speech. These laws protect Jewish and other minority residents and show that societies clearly value their safety and security in their countries. These laws have not prevented all acts of racism and violence from occurring, as the Charlie Hebdo attacks in France remind us, but they send the right message to vulnerable minorities and galvanize public and police support to prevent future atrocities.

If the Oklahoma chant happened in, say, Germany and the n-word was replaced with a derogatory epithet for the Jewish people, and the method of murder was changed from lynching to something employed by the Nazis, the perpetrators would be in jail right now and few outside the extremist right would argue that an injustice was done. How can so many in American society condone this incitement as youthful indiscretion and even redirect blame away from the perpetrators to the people who have had to suffer the oppression inflicted by those who spew these vile words?

America can learn something from the international community, where the legacy and dangers of certain types of speech are better understood. We too must find an effective way to monitor and forbid dangerous speech, without unjustly infringing upon freedom of speech. We should have started the discussion long ago.

No Matter How Unwelcome, Sexually Explicit Speech Is Not Sexual Assault

Nadine Strossen and Tom Patterson

Nadine Strossen served as president of the American Civil Liberties Union (ACLU) for eighteen years and is currently a professor of Law at New York Law School. Tom Patterson is acting director of the Shorenstein Center on Media, Politics and Public Policy at Harvard University.

I've chosen to focus on another ongoing free speech challenge, which is even closer to home for all of us here, namely, I'm going to discuss one of the many rampant free speech problems we've been facing on campuses all over the US, including right here at Harvard. I'm grateful to many members of the Harvard community who have stood up for free speech here and beyond. Now, I'd like to salute just one such free speech champion who is with us tonight, one of my guests, Harvey Silverglate who is a Harvard Law School alum, who co-founded a very important organization, FIRE, the Foundation for Individual Rights in Education, and is also a long time ACLU leader.

Earlier this year, University of Chicago adopted a powerful re-commitment to campus free speech, precisely to push back against the prevailing suppression. The statement was drafted by UC's acting Law School dean, Geoff Stone, who has been a free speech scholar and advocate for almost half a century. Yet, Geoff recently said, "the level of intolerance for controversial views on college campuses today is much greater than at any time in my memory." And I concur with that.

Of the many current free speech problems, the one I've chosen to address in my brief time is one that Harvey Silverglate

"Free Expression: An Endangered Species on Campus?" by Nadine Strossen, Shorenstein Center, November 5, 2015. https://shorensteincenter.org/nadine-strossen-free-expression-an-endangered-species-on-campus-transcript/. Licensed under CC BY-ND 3.0. Copyright © 2018 Shorenstein Center.

complained about specifically at Harvard Law School, way back in 1996 in a *Wall Street Journal* op-ed. And it's a general problem that I wrote about even earlier, in my 1995 book, *Defending Pornography*.

Sadly though, this problem has become even worse since then. Specifically, I'm referring to the overbroad, unjustified concept of illegal sexual harassment as extending to speech with any sexual content that anyone finds offensive. This distorted concept has recently become entrenched on campus due to pressure from the Department of Education's Office of Civil Rights, the OCR. By threatening to pull federal funds, the OCR has forced schools, even well-endowed schools such as Harvard, to adopt sexual misconduct policies that violate many civil liberties, as denounced by an admirable, remarkable open letter that 28 members of the Harvard Law School faculty published last fall, with the signers including distinguished female professors who are lifelong feminist scholars and women's rights advocates.

Tonight, I'm going to be zeroing in on just one of these problematic sexual misconduct policies, namely, as I said, the sexual harassment concept, because its subversion of free speech is germane to the theme of this lecture series.

Of course, combating gender discrimination, violence and sexual assault is of the utmost urgency. I hope that goes without saying, but I will underscore it: of the utmost urgency.

But, OCR's distorted concept of sexual harassment actually does more harm than good to gender justice, not to mention to free speech. More than 20 years ago, my book, *Defending Pornography*, made this point in the context of opposing laws that some feminists were then advocating, laws that would ban sexual expression that they viewed as demeaning to women. In fact, there was a vigorous campaign for one such law right here in Cambridge, which was defeated, thanks in large part, to other anti-censorship feminists, including the Boston Women's Health Collective, the publishers of the classic, *Our Bodies Ourselves*.

Well, alas, all these years later, decades later, my book's message is still relevant in response to the still ongoing efforts to suppress sexual expression for the purported sake of women's equality and safety, now through the vehicle of campus sexual harassment policies.

By the way, this book was my first non-academic publication. And I hadn't realized how few free speech rights first-time authors have in their contracts with major publishers. So, I didn't have much to say over the book's title or cover, which the publisher clearly designed to be in your face, provocative. You see that subtitle, *Free Speech, Sex, and the Fight for Women's Rights*. And then, that neon, flaming, big word, "pornography" right in the middle. Well, that prompted this comment from one of my academic friends, who had written scholarly works on the general subject with the typical long, dull academic titles, you know, with a semicolon in the middle, and dripping with sarcasm, and maybe a little envy, she said, "Gee, Nadine, couldn't they work in the word orgasm, too?"

OCR's flawed sexual harassment concept reflects sexist stereotypes that are equally insulting to women and men. For women, it embodies the archaic and infantilizing notion that we are inherently demeaned by any expression with sexual content.

And that same problem plagued the anti-pornography laws that I mentioned. In fact, the ACLU's lawsuits against those anti-pornography laws argued that they violated both free speech and gender equality.

I'd like to quote a brief that the ACLU Women's Rights Project filed more than 30 years ago, which sadly is fully apt today. "A law that equates women with children and men with satyrs is hardly a step toward gender equality."

Shortly after Ruth Bader Ginsberg became the founding Director of the ACLU Women's Rights Project in 1972, a reporter who was interviewing her used a somewhat belittling term from that era, describing her work as "women's lib," to which Ginsberg sternly retorted, "No. We're working to liberate men and women."

And here I want to draw another important lesson from that classic liberal concept of gender justice, as even the detractors recognized through that flip term lib, the key goal was liberation, liberty. In contrast, when I read what is self-proclaimed as feminism on campus today, too often the new watch word has become something diametrically different, namely safety.

Let me quote my favorite rebuttal to this fearful approach. It comes from one of the greatest Supreme Court opinions ever, happens to be a First Amendment opinion, very fitting for this occasion. And I'm referring to Justice Brandeis's 1927 opinion in *Whitney v. [California]*. He wrote, "Those who want our independence believed that the final end of the state was to make us free. They believed liberty to be the secret of happiness and courage to be the secret of liberty."

There's yet a further problem with the current campus exultation of safety, namely, it's very different from the dictionary definition. Rather, the current clamor for campus safety seeks protection from exposure to ideas that make one uncomfortable.

For instance, last fall, Brown University set up a safe space for students who felt endangered by the mere fact that a debate was taking place on campus on the topic of how should colleges handle sexual assault.

Let me quote the *New York Times* article on point. "The room was equipped with cookies, coloring books, bubbles, play dough, calming music, pillows, blankets and a video of frolicking puppies, as well as students and staff members trained to deal with trauma. Emma Hall, a junior, went to the debate. But, she said that after a while, she had to go to the safe space, because 'I was feeling bombarded by a lot of viewpoints that really go against my dearly and closely held beliefs.'"

This focus on safety from disturbing ideas is especially misplaced given the ongoing serious threats to students' physical safety on campus, including rape and sexual assault, which continue to be alarmingly prevalent, as indicated by a survey that the Association of American Universities released just a couple of weeks ago. And I saw President Faust's follow on letter to the Harvard community about that.

And also, in the wake of the latest mass gun murders on campus just last Thursday, less than a week ago, we have to contrast government's pressure to shield students from ideas with its failure to shield them from guns. To the contrary, some laws are even moving in the opposite direction. For example, Texas has enacted a so-called campus concealed carry law which actually allows gun owners to bring their hidden weapons into the classroom. Think what that's going to do for open debate in a classroom.

In short, when it comes to safety, our students are being doubly disserved. Too often, denied safety from physical violence, which is critical for their education, but too often granted safety from ideas, which is antithetical to their education.

To say that we should be protected from any idea is the exact opposite of what the Supreme Court has held as the bedrock of our free speech system. Namely that speech may never be suppressed because anyone had any negative reaction to its ideas—even the most vehemently negative reaction by even the vast majority of our fellow citizens. To be sure, speech may be suppressed if, but only if, it poses an imminent danger of concrete injury, for example, an intentional incitement of imminent violence.

However, short of such an extraordinary situation, Justice Brandeis eloquently explains why we must brave the discomforts and other potential downsides that are posed by speech whose ideas we consider evil and even incendiary.

As he said, "Fear of serious injury cannot alone justify suppression of free speech. Men feared witches and burned women. The fitting remedy for evil counsels is good ones."

This speech protective philosophy was memorably summed up specifically in the campus context by a revered past university president, Clark Kerr of the University of California. As he said, "The University is not engaged in making ideas safe for students. It is engaged in making students safe for ideas."

Now, when Kerr uttered these bracing words in 1961, it was the students who were fighting for freedom and government officials who sought to stifle freedom in the name of safety. Alas, this situation has been inverted on too many campuses today with students themselves asking the university, demanding the university to keep them safe from disturbing ideas.

In response, university officials could well quote a point Dick Salant used to make about the broadcast media. As he said, "Our job is to give people not what they want, but what we decide they ought to have."

Notably, in 1984, Harvard President, Derek Bok, quoted Clark Kerr's great line in an eloquent open letter Bok wrote to the Harvard community about various free speech controversies that had recently roiled this campus. This letter remains fully apt today. And I was happy to see it's actually posted on the Harvard website, along with some other policies that are less speech friendly. Let diversity bloom, I guess.

One of the incidents that Bok described was a flyer that a Harvard fraternity had circulated which, to quote him, "Referred to women in terms that were lewd, insulting and grossly demeaning." While he stressed that this speech should not be penalized in any iota at all, he also explained that it should be publicly condemned. And I'd like to summarize this key distinction by saying that we should not censor offensive speech, but we surely have a responsibility to censure it, and I think Bok sets a marvelous example.

Now, I'll explain in a bit more detail the free speech and feminist laws with OCR's sexual harassment concept which Harvard and too many other schools have adopted. Again, the OCR has forced campuses to punish as sexual harassment "any unwelcome conduct of a sexual nature." There is no exception for speech. To the contrary, the OCR definition expressly extends to "verbal conduct" which is a good example of Orwellian newspeak. Or I should say, it's a good example of Orwellian new verbal conduct.

In short, campuses are pressured to punish as harassment any expression with any sexual content that anyone subjectively finds offensive, no matter how unreasonably or irrationally. And the OCR explicitly rejected an objective reasonable person standard, stating that "expression will be harassing, even if it is not offensive to an objectively reasonable person of the same gender in the same situation."

As a nice coincidence, one of the first critiques of this censorial concept was written by none other than journalist Michael Barone, the widower of Joan Shorenstein, the remarkable namesake of the Shorenstein Center. Michael Barone denounced the OCR rule shortly after it had been announced in 2011 in a column he wrote which was referring to a then current political scandal that some of you might remember. As he wrote, "This sexual harassment concept could get campus speakers into big trouble for saying something considerably milder than the double entendres we were hearing in cable news coverage of the Anthony Weiner scandal."

Universities have, in fact, been punishing students and faculty members for all manner of sexually themed expression, even when it has an important academic purpose. The most egregious, most recent example is the prolonged sexual harassment investigation that Northwestern University conducted against film professor Laura Kipnis earlier this year because of an article she published in the *Chronicle of Higher Education*, in which, ironically, she criticized the exaggerated, distorted concept of sexual harassment that is prevalent on campus.

For months, the university subjected her to Star Chamber type interrogations pursuing the charge that her essay somehow constituted unlawful harassment.

I'd like to cite just a few other examples of campus censorship in the guise of punishing sexual harassment. The Naval War College placed a professor on administrative leave and demanded he apologize because, during a lecture that critically described Machiavelli's views about leadership, he paraphrased Machiavelli's comments about raping the goddess Fortuna.

Another example: The University of Denver suspended a tenured professor and found him guilty of sexual harassment for teaching about sexual topics in a graduate-level course in the course unit entitled "Drugs and Sin in American Life from Masturbation and Prostitution to Alcohol and Drugs."

Next example: A sociology professor at Appalachian State University was suspended because she showed a documentary film that critically examined the adult film industry.

A sociology professor at the University of Colorado was forced to retire early because of a class in her course on deviance in which volunteer student assistants played roles in a scripted skit about prostitution.

A professor of English and film studies at San Bernardino Valley College was punished for requiring his class to write essays defining pornography. Yes, that was just defining it, not even defending it.

And just this summer, Louisiana State University fired a tenured professor of early childhood education who has received multiple teaching awards, because she occasionally used vulgar language and humor about sex when she was teaching about sexuality and also to capture her students' attention. And I could go on. You get the idea.

Now, I'd like to underscore why we should not punish any unwelcome sexual speech as the OCR dictates. In our wonderfully diverse society, we all have widely divergent views about what sexual expression we find positive or negative. I'd like to describe a cartoon en pointe. It shows three people in an art museum looking at a classic nude female torso, a fragment of an ancient sculpture minus the head and minus the limbs. And each viewer's reaction is shown in an air bubble. And the first one thinks, art. And the second one thinks, smut. And the third one thinks, an insult to amputees.

We individuals even have different perspectives about whether any given expression has any sexual content at all. That's captured by the old joke about the man who sees every ink blot his psychiatrist shows him as wildly erotic. And when the psychiatrist says to him, you're obsessed with sex, the man answers, what do you mean I'm obsessed? You're the one who keeps showing me all these dirty pictures.

In short, we individuals cannot delegate these inherently subjective determinations to any officials. As with all discretionary decisions, they will be arbitrary at best, discriminatory at worst.

An appropriately limited concept of illegal sexual harassment in the educational context was issued by the Supreme Court in 1999. And by the way, one of the points that was made in this remarkable open letter by the 28 Harvard Law School faculty members was that of the definition of sexual harassment that this school, among many others, has adopted under pressure of the OCR, departs from and is inconsistent with the Supreme Court's definition.

And here is how the Supreme Court defines it: Not just anything that anyone considers unwelcome, subjectively as the OCR would have it, but rather, only unwelcomed conduct that is targeted, discriminatory and—I'm going to quote—"so severe, pervasive and objectively offensive, and that so undermines and detracts from the victim's educational experience, that the victims are effectively denied equal access to an institution's resources and opportunities."

Now that concept respects both free speech and gender equality. And therefore, it's been endorsed by advocates of both, including the ACLU Women's Rights Project and the AAUP, the American Association of University Professors Committee on Women in the Academic Profession.

Indeed, in the teaching context, the AAUP advocates an added prerequisite before any expression may be deemed to be sexual harassment, namely that it is not germane to the subject matter, an additional requirement. And here's AAUP's explanation for that—and it's specifically their Committee on Women in the Academic Profession: "The academic setting is distinct from the work place in that, wide latitude is required for professional judgment in determining the appropriate content and presentation of academic material."

Unfortunately, Harvard is just one of the growing number of campuses that has been pressured to adopt the OCR's dangerously distorted concept of sexual harassment. And this has had a chilling effect here, according to one of your leading in house critics, somebody I greatly admire, but I'm in broad company, because she's an internationally renowned feminist scholar and activist, namely

Harvard Law School professor Janet Halley. Let me quote from a trenchant critique that she published in *The Crimson* last year. "To the OCR, academic freedom, the very lifeblood of education and research, appears not to register as important at all. Classroom instruction and academic debate can and will become the basis of complaints and sanctions. Chill is already happening. Teachers at Harvard alarmed by the policy's expansive scope are jettisoning teaching tools that make any reference to human sexuality."

Well, I'm running out of time. I would like to close on a positive note, so let me quote on that point, one of my favorite philosophers, Woody Allen. He was once coming to the end of a speech and he told the audience, "I want to end with something positive, but I can't think of anything positive to say. Would you settle for two negatives?"

I can cite many positives. And first and foremost, the many individuals at Harvard and elsewhere who are courageously standing up for free speech, including by resisting OCR overreach. You are acting in the finest traditions that were set by Dick Salant and Frank Stanton. Thank you very much.

Words Are Not Equal to Violence

Josh Craddock

Josh Craddock is the Vice President of Personhood USA, a human rights organization devoted to protecting every human being as a person, by love and by law. Between 2011 and 2014, he managed advocacy teams for several nonprofit organizations at the United Nations, promoting life and family values during negotiations for the Sustainable Development Goals. He is currently a student at Harvard Law School.

*S**ticks and stones may break my bones, but words will never hurt me.* The childish playground ditty is at least partly true: Mere words cannot break an arm or bust a nose. Words can be hurtful emotionally and psychologically, but they cannot be acts of violence because they lack physicality.

Some academics and journalists need this reminder. In the pages of the *New York Times*, Amanda Hess claims that "America is struggling to sort out where violence begins and ends." She dignifies the theory that "violence is embedded in everything from our social structures to our speech—that speech itself can *be* a form of violence, one every bit as meaningful as the physical kind."

This concept is already dominant on college campuses, thanks to its propagation within feminist-studies programs influenced by Judith Butler. Social psychologist Jonathan Haidt, remarking on a recent Berkeley student-newspaper article defending rioters who burnt their campus to stop Milo Yiannopoulos from speaking, observes that students use the word "violence" to denote "words that have a negative effect on members of the sacred victim groups. And so it even follows that silence can be violence."

Lisa Feldman Barrett tries to clothe the emperor's nakedness with a veil of respectability in her own *Times* op-ed, "When is speech violence?" The result is comical. She argues, without a whiff of irony, that because offensive words can cause stress, and "prolonged stress can cause physical harm, then it seems that speech—at least certain types of speech—can be a form of violence." By that logic, of course, being evicted is also a form of violence, since eviction causes prolonged stress.

Despite its ivory-tower proponents, the speech-violence theory should be rejected as both ignorant and dangerous.

I say ignorant because it does violence to language (metaphorically speaking). By definition, violence involves physical force. *Merriam-Webster* defines the term as "exertion of physical force so as to injure or abuse." *The Oxford English Dictionary* calls it "the deliberate exercise of physical force against a person, property, etc.; physically violent behaviour or treatment." In secondary definitions, the OED observes that violence can be applied descriptively to powerful natural forces, or analogically to intense expressions of emotion or behavior. It attributes the etymology to the Latin *violentus*, meaning use of force, especially destructive force.

From these we may ascertain different senses of the term's usage. We might say that one speaks violently to describe the manner or delivery of a speaker's message. We might call words violent when their semantic content is particularly gory or grotesque. But words cannot themselves be *acts* of violence, even if everyone knows that words can *inspire* violence. (A fine line should be drawn between violent acts inspired by speech and the expression itself.)

Speech-violence theories are dangerous because they undermine free-speech norms, which are central to a political life of civic republicanism and virtuous self-government. If utterances of speech are truly violence, then government can ban them as criminal conduct, just as we prohibit other forms of private violence.

Take "misgendering" as an example. Transgender TV star Laverne Cox has said that "misgendering a transgendered person" is "an act of violence." Another transgender activist, Riley Dennis, argues that common dictionary definitions of violence such as those I examined above are "outdated," and that "violence" includes "all types of societal power imbalances" that might cause "psychological harm" by making a transgendered person "feel bad." Nora Berenstain, an assistant professor of philosophy at the University of Tennessee, adds that using words and phrases like "transgenderism," "male genitalia," and "biological sex" is also a form of "discursive transmisogynistic violence." And on and on it goes.

If "misgendering" is an act of violence, then New York City's speech code imposing staggering fines for "incorrect" pronoun usage is legitimate. Under the Orwellian theory of speech-violence, refusing to endorse a controversial anthropological claim about the nature of human sexuality constitutes violence, no different from punching an ideological opponent in the face. The same speech-violence theory underlies France's decision to criminalize expression that exerts "psychological and moral pressure" on women considering abortion.

Of course, such an elastic definition neuters violence of any coherent meaning. Anything resulting from what social-justice advocates label a "power imbalance"—which according to their dogma is just about everything—would then be considered "violence." Set aside for a moment the question of whether identifying an individual using pronouns that correspond to his or her biological sex or expressing moral disapproval of abortion actually causes psychological harm. The notion that words that make people "feel bad" are acts of violence is frighteningly capacious.

What government bureaucracy can be trusted to discern which instances of speech rise to the level of "violence"? A circumspect evaluation of human frailty and partisanship should be a stark warning to those would entrust government with that authority.

If words that make people feel bad are violence, then people who are offended would be justified in using physical force as a means of self-defense. Some masked campus radicals already cheer this notion, and welcome it as a convenient excuse to go on riotous rampages to stop controversial speakers from invading their safe spaces with ideas they dislike. Those who care about the free exchange of ideas have cause for concern.

Rather than proscribe uncouth or impolitic speech as violence, Americans should heed Justice Brandeis's wise words from *Whitney v. California*, which recall the original purpose of constitutionally guaranteed freedom of speech:

> Those who won our independence ... believed that freedom to think as you will and to speak as you think are means indispensable to the discovery and spread of political truth; that, without free speech and assembly, discussion would be futile; that, with them, discussion affords ordinarily adequate protection against the dissemination of noxious doctrine; that the greatest menace to freedom is an inert people; that public discussion is a political duty, and that this should be a fundamental principle of the American government. They recognized the risks to which all human institutions are subject. But they knew that ... fear breeds repression; that repression breeds hate; that hate menaces stable government; that the path of safety lies in the opportunity to discuss freely supposed grievances and proposed remedies, and that the fitting remedy for evil counsels is good ones. Believing in the power of reason as applied through public discussion, they eschewed silence coerced by law—the argument of force in its worst form. Recognizing the occasional tyrannies of governing majorities, they amended the Constitution so that free speech and assembly should be guaranteed.

CHAPTER 4

Should Speech on Campus Be Regulated More Than Other Public Speech?

The Conflict Between Free Speech Absolutists and Skeptics Has Reached Its Peak

Mary Ellen Flannery

Mary Ellen Flannery is Senior Writer/Editor at the National Education Association. Prior to her tenure at NEA, she was a reporter for the Miami Herald *and the* Palm Beach Post.

Last month, after violent clashes with more than 100 masked protesters, University of California, Berkeley canceled an appearance by Milo Yiannapoulos, a notorious commentator who was banned from Twitter for his hate-filled speech. In March, a professor at Middlebury College ended up with a concussion while escorting Charles Murray, the author of *The Bell Curve*, a book that claims Black people are genetically inferior, through an angry mob.

These incidents prompt faculty, staff and students to ask: What happens when the good thing that is academic freedom runs into the bad thing that is hate speech? "This issue is as important as it ever has been," said Gary Rhoades, director of the Center for the Study of Higher Education at the University of Arizona, to an audience at the National Education Association's Higher Education Conference on March 18.

"There is this dance between academic freedom and the legitimate concerns of specific groups about the climate of the institutions where they work and study," says Rhoades. "The question is, how do we protect academic freedom, especially during this era of 'you're fired,' and also meet the goals of greater inclusion and openness in the academy?"

NEA's resolution on academic freedom is nearly 90 years old. At its heart is the idea that the pursuit of truth on campuses serves a

"Conflict Between Free Speech and Hate Speech Hits Boiling Point on College Campuses," by Mary Ellen Flannery, National Education Association, March 20, 2017. Reprinted by permission.

common good in society. It's this kind of thinking that has allowed scientists to explore the melting polar ice caps, or historians to delve in the causes of war. Over the decades, NEA's resolution has been updated, but it has never wavered from "the rights of teachers and learners to explore and discuss divergent points of view."

On many campuses, protecting these rights is the work of unions, which often negotiate and embed academic freedom into faculty contracts. (These types of contract language are explored in a recent *NEA Almanac of Higher Education* article.) Kristine Anderson Dougherty, a former chief negotiator for the United Faculty of Florida, points to the University of New Hampshire contract for typical language: "The College cannot fulfill its purpose of transmitting, evaluating and extending knowledge if it requires conformity with any orthodoxy of content and/ or method."

Free Speech vs. Hate Speech

But times are changing. The election of President Trump has invited the haters to take the stage, writes Allison Stanger, the Middlebury professor who was attacked on her campus. "Much of the free speech he has inspired—or has refused to disavow—is ugly, and has already had ugly real-world consequences."

Meanwhile, our institutions are becoming more diverse, like our country, and students of color, students who are immigrants, LGBT students, and others, need to feel welcome and supported to succeed. It's impossible to feel that way when the speaker on the campus stage talks about the transgender bathroom debate, displays a photo of a transgender student at that school, and then tells the crowd, "the way that you know he's failing is that I'd almost still bang him."

But who and what do you censor in the name of student safety? Different campuses have responded in different ways. At the University of Oregon in December, a law professor was suspended for wearing blackface to a Halloween party at her home—a costume she said she intended as a pro-Black statement, but that some students in attendance found offensive and the university called an act of "harassment."

"Last week, the University of Oregon made clear to its faculty: If you say things about race, sexual orientation, sex, religion and so on that enough people find offensive, you could get suspended... even fired," wrote Eugene Volokh in the *Washington Post*. Following this logic, he continues, "the expression of certain views, however linked they may be to important political debates, is forbidden to University of Oregon professors, at least once the views create enough controversy."

At Washington State University, some professors published an open letter in December, calling on their campus to assert "we are anti-racist, anti-sexist, anti-xenophobia, anti-homophobic, anti-Islamophobic, anti-ableism, and anti-bigotry." It seemed to warn again too much free speech, saying "discourses of free speech undeviatingly create a campus that is especially disempowering to marginalized students."

But what about academic freedom, and the pursuit of truth? Entering the fray last week, an ideological odd couple—conservative intellectual Robert George of Princeton University and self-described "radical Democrat" Cornel West of Harvard—issued a joint statement. "When George and West agree on something and lend their names to it, people take notice," wrote an *Inside Higher Ed* reporter.

Their statement, which has received tens of thousands of signatures of support, calls for "truth seeking, democracy and freedom of thought and expression." And while it acknowledges the rights of students to "peacefully protest," by turning their backs to speakers, for example, it asks, "Might it better serve the cause of truth-seeking to engage the speaker in frank civil discussion?"

These are fine words, but they may not reflect the reality in our public colleges and universities, suggests Rhoades. "There has been an upsurge in hate crimes. There has been an upsurge in sexual assaults. We must address that as a faculty and not just say, no, don't infringe on our academic freedom!"

For his part, Rhoades recommends joint labor-management task forces to explore these issues on campuses, "and work together to advance healthier campuses."

Universities Should Be Able to Enforce Speech Norms to Maintain the Stability of Their Community

Scott Bomboy

Scott Bomboy is the editor of Digital Content and Operations at the National Constitution Center in Philadelphia.

When and where can students and members of the public express their free-speech rights at public universities? These First Amendment rights are limited and differ greatly based on policies set by colleges and state lawmakers.

News reports about free speech restrictions at schools and a desire of some public universities to keep their "free-speech zones" have led to a lot of debate, and a few lawsuits, in recent years. In March 2017, Kevin Shaw, a student at Pierce College in California, sued the public community college when he was prevented from handing out Spanish-language copies of the Constitution by an administrator. Shaw was not in a college-designated free-speech zone at the time and didn't have a school-endorsed permit to solicit literature.

Pierce College's policies stated that it considered the campus a "non-public forum" except for areas designated as "free speech areas" with a normal flow of student traffic, Shaw's attorneys said in a lawsuit filed in federal court.

The Foundation for Individual Rights in Education (or FIRE), a Philadelphia-based First Amendment advocacy group, is representing Shaw along with a law firm. FIRE said the free-speech area represented 616 square feet on a 426 acre campus, and claimed the Pierce College free-speech policy was clearly unconstitutional.

FIRE has won in court in similar cases. In 2014, it represented a student at Citrus College in California who won a

"The boundaries of free speech at public colleges," by Scott Bomboy, National Constitution Center, August 16, 2017. Reprinted by permission.

$110,000 settlement after school officials wouldn't let him solicit a petition protesting government surveillance because he was outside of a free-speech zone. Back in March, when *USA Today* covered Shaw's suit, FIRE told the newspaper that 10 percent of the 450 colleges and universities it tracks have free-speech zones.

While Shaw's case involves a student claiming a free-speech violation, not only students have free-speech rights on public university property. Outside groups with strong, controversial messages such as the Westboro Baptist Church, have appeared on college campuses. (Guests who also speak about provocative topics, if invited on campus by a school or through a facility rental program, have similar rights.)

The subject of free-speech zones on campus remains a sore point. The zones started during the Vietnam War era, when universities needed a way to safely contain anti-war protests. Some states and public universities are either eliminating free-speech zones or scaling back their use. North Carolina, Tennessee and Arizona recently passed laws that protect the rights of speakers of all viewpoints and restrict the use of free-speech zones. But some of these laws include sanctions against people who interrupt the First Amendment rights of speakers on campus.

Thomas Harnisch, director of state relations and policy analysis at the American Association of State Colleges and Universities, told *USA Today* in July that there are concerns about the laws being politically motivated and infringing on the traditional rights of schools to ensure a safe environment. "These bills are not uniform, and they range from being relatively benign to redundant while others are very prescriptive and micromanage campuses. Some of these bills could be dangerous in the sense that they could tie the hands of campuses in their efforts to protect the physical safety of those on campus," he said.

And the issue came up in Congress in June at a Senate Judiciary Committee hearing on the First Amendment at college campuses.

Eugene Volokh, a UCLA law professor, told the committee that the interchange between First Amendment speakers on campus was important. "The First Amendment doesn't require public universities to protect speakers from being shouted down or even attacked. It does bar public universities from protecting some speakers based on viewpoint but denying such protection to others; but when a university wants to let hecklers and thugs generally control what is said on campus, that is not itself a First Amendment violation. Yet it is an abdication of the universities' responsibility to foster free discussion," Volokh said.

And Floyd Abrams, the noted First Amendment attorney, told the Senate panel that while such debates can be painful that were useful and had remedies.

"The answer to the suppression of almost any speech, the First Amendment answer, cannot be to limit expression but to discuss it, not to bar offensive speech but to answer it. Or to ignore it. Or to persuade the public to reject it. I know that's easy to say but it's got to be the way we respond to speech which we abhor. What is unacceptable is to suppress the speech."

Certain Restrictions on Speech Can Support Feelings of Safety and Acceptance for Marginalized Groups

PEN America

PEN America champions the freedom of writers and publishers. Their mission is to unite writers and their allies to celebrate creative expression and defend the liberties that make it possible.

[...]

Title IX's Current Approach to Harassment and Speech as an Essential Tool to Combat Rampant Rates of Harassment

The Department of Education's approach to speech and harassment has its defenders. Advocates for aggressive enforcement of Title IX point to the shocking prevalence of sexual violence and discrimination on campus to justify the need for intense vigilance against even early manifestations of conduct that could evolve into harassment. A public white paper issued by prominent law professors and scholars in support of the OCR's recent actions began by noting that "three decades of research showing epidemic levels of sexual harassment at colleges and universities"[1] is sufficient to validate robust enforcement, arguing that: "If the 2011 DCL came as a surprise to any school it could only have been because that school had not been paying attention either to what OCR had been regulating as sexual harassment or to what was happening on its own campus."[2]

The white paper described the long-term harms suffered by survivors of sexual violence and harassment—especially those re-victimized by schools failing to provide them with proper support and access to justice:

> Evidence shows that many victims are at serious risk of experiencing a downward spiral of damaging health, educational

"And Campus For All: Diversity, Inclusion, and Freedom of Speech at U.S. Universities," Pages 30-31. PEN America, October 2016. Reprinted by permission.

and economic effects ... The cost that school cultures of masculine sexual aggression and entitlement impose on women, girls and gender minorities compel action, and we applaud the OCR for taking such action. Indeed, as an Office for Civil Rights, OCR must act to redress injuries that such a culture disproportionately inflicts on certain groups of students based on gender and various intersectional, multidimensional identities (emphasis in original).[3]

A number of prominent feminist university professors have also challenged the AAUP report's assessment that Title IX investigations jeopardize free speech. Faculty Against Rape, an ad hoc association with more than 300 professors and civil rights activists, released a public letter criticizing the AAUP report for factual and legal errors and disputing its central contention that the OCR is conflating protected speech and sexual harassment:

We believe that the AAUP's claim that the OCR's 2011 DCL "conflates conduct and speech" is a misinterpretation. The 2011 DCL never uses the word "speech" and only uses the word "verbal" in connection with "conduct of a sexual nature." AAUP also claims that it refers to a speech-based hostile environment when it does not. However, it makes us wonder if the authors of the report think that evaluations of alleged sexual harassment should never consider the verbal component of conduct, in the interest of protecting free speech and academic freedom. That would obviously be a very problematic stance. Not all forms of speech conduct are protected in this way under the law.[4]

The letter also pointed out a serious concern relating to free expression that was not addressed in the AAUP report, namely high rates of retaliation against those who report instances of campus rape and assault, deterring those who fear a loss of job security or other benefits from speaking out. Campuses concerned about legal liability and public reputations can discourage reporting as well.[5]

The OCR directly addressed, and dismissed, the criticism

that its enforcement policies infringed on academic freedom and speech. In an April 2014 "Frequently Asked Questions" document relating to sexual violence, it wrote:

> When a school works to prevent and redress discrimination, it must respect the free-speech rights of students, faculty, and other speakers. Title IX protects students from sex discrimination; it does not regulate the content of speech. OCR recognizes that the offensiveness of a particular expression as perceived by some students, standing alone, is not a legally sufficient basis to establish a hostile environment under Title IX.[6]

In the view of Title IX defenders, rather than being guilty of administrative overreach and the chilling of speech, the OCR is simply fulfilling its statutory mandate.

The National Women's Law Center has complained that the OCR "is facing unwarranted criticism for doing its job" to redress the disturbing prevalence of sex-based discrimination on campuses and urged "the Department to continue helping schools understand their legal obligations."[7]

To make matters worse, these critics point out that OCR's budget has been slashed in half since 1980 while student complaints have tripled. This has created a large backlog of cases and heightened the imperative of transferring the onus of policing harassment from the OCR to the universities themselves, as well as the need to emphasize prevention. The OCR sets a goal to complete cases within 180 days, but in 2014 the average time to resolve a complaint was 1,469 days, up from 379 days in 2009.[8] As the white paper points out:

> OCR is not initiating these complaints—victims are. At times, critics of the 2011 DCL seem to suggest that OCR has created a problem that schools must then solve, but the problem originates at the schools themselves. The problems is the thousands of students who are assaulted and harassed each year, and who feel re-victimized by their institutions' handling of their complaints, and who then, logically, ask the office charged with ensuring equal educational opportunity to help them and students like

them to find redress.[9]

In fact, some advocates call for OCR to expand rather than limit its mandate, arguing that the severity and pervasiveness of harassment, particularly in light of new social media platforms, warrant broad and aggressive measures that should not be forestalled by concerns over free speech.[10] An October 20 letter sent by more than 50 women's rights, gay rights, and other civil rights groups to then–secretary of Education Arne Duncan and his deputy for civil rights complained that "many schools have shirked these legal obligations by citing vague First Amendment concerns."[11]

> The letter urged measures to intensify the application of Title IX, particularly to target social media sites such as Yik Yak that allow users to post anonymously. The letter stated that these applications were being used to: harass, threaten, and attack their peers while hiding behind a perceived shield of anonymity. So far, academic institutions have not adequately responded to this new phenomenon, essentially allowing students to engage in sex- and race-based harassment that would otherwise be prohibited by Title IX and Title VI.[12]

[...]

Notes

1. "Title IX and the Preponderance of the Evidence," White Paper (Signed by Over 90 Law Professors), http://bit.ly/2cLEcpz, 3-4. [hereinafter White Paper]

2. Ibid.

3. Id, 1, 3. A letter organized by the National Women's Law Center and signed by dozens of women's rights organizations also warns of the significant long-term damage caused by the failure of universities to provide a safe environment for students: "sex-based harassment can be very damaging to the lives of women and girls, both in its emotional impact and in its impact on their education. Feeling unsafe at school has been correlated with declining academic performance, skipping school, and dropping out." "The Next Generation of Title IX: Harassment and Bullying Based on Sex," *National Women's Law Center*, June 2012, http://bit.ly/2dl3OLb

4. "Letter to American Association of University Professors," Faculty Against Rape, April 15, 2016, 5, http://bit.ly/2daDzVr [hereinafter FAR Letter).

6. "Questions and Answers on Title IX and Sexual Violence," *United States Department of Education Office for Civil Rights*, http://bit.ly/2dFsGKZ [hereinafter USDoE, "Title IX and Sexual Violence"]

7. "Sign-on Letter Supporting Title IX Guidance and Enforcement," *National Women's Law Center*, July 13, 2016, http://bit.ly/2daDzVr

8. Jake New, "Justice Delayed," *Inside Higher Education*, May 6, 2015, http://bit.ly/2cGvw5f

9. Id.

10. White Paper, 12.

11. Dia Kayyali and Danny O'Brien, "Facing the Challenge of Online Harassment", *Electronic Frontier Foundation*, January 8, 2015, http://bit.ly/1487vur

12. Re: Request for Guidance Reminding Schools of Obligations Under Title IX and Title VI to Address Sex- and Race-Based Harassment Occurring on Yik Yak and Other Anonymous Social Media Applications, October 20, 2015, http://bit.ly/2ddhHNb

Common Sense Limits on Free Speech Are Necessary for Public Schools in America

Center for Public Education

The Center for Public Education is a national resource for accurate, timely, and credible information about public education and its importance to the well-being of our nation. The Center provides up-to-date research, data, and analysis on current education issues and explores ways to improve student achievement and engage public support for public schools.

Students and teachers are free to speak their minds on public school grounds. They can even wear T-shirts with messages, dye their hair funky colors, and wear jewelry or buttons that make a social statement. But, even with First Amendment protection guaranteed by the US Constitution, there are limits in the school setting. And figuring out where the line is drawn is fairly complicated.

The reason is that the First Amendment's Free Speech Clause requires courts and school districts to weigh and balance two forceful ideas that occasionally clash:

- The need for a safe, orderly school environment conducive to learning.
- The guaranteed American entitlement to speak or engage in expressive activity.

Neither interest is trivial. Words and symbols are at the core of American society, and free speech, many believe, separates the United States from oppressive countries. Public schools are society in miniature, with students and school employees representing the full range of beliefs.

It is important to remember that speech, as defined by the Constitution, is not just words. It also includes non-verbal

"Free speech and public schools," Center for Public Education, National School Boards Association. Reprinted by permission.

and symbolic expression: clothes, off-campus web sites, dance performances, and art. In today's climate, questions about freedom of speech are amplified. The nation is polarized by matters of war and peace, and in-your-face moral issues provoke car discussions that make parents cringe.

Part of the mission of public schools is to teach children what democracy is all about. Tax-supported schools are also, by their actions, examples of democracy in action. It would be the height of contradiction to teach about the First Amendment and then not follow it. Yet, free speech cannot trump the main mission. As one federal court put it, "Learning is more important in the classroom than free speech."

Free Speech as a Public School Guidepost

While the US Constitution applies within schools, rights are slightly reduced for the following reasons:

- Students are minors.
- Adults serve as employees.
- A public learning institution requires a peaceful environment to thrive.

Public schools are in a category all their own. They must achieve academic excellence while obeying various laws, rules, and regulations. Private and parochial schools, however, are not similarly restricted by ideas of individual rights, free speech, and other liberties. Further, non-public learning places can trample on freedoms with impunity and never face a date in court.

The big idea behind free speech is simply this: Students and teachers are free to reveal their views unless there is a compelling reason to stop it. School officials cannot arbitrarily pick and choose the speech it will allow.

The following examples illustrate this conflict.

OK: Allowing a student to wear a T-shirt that says "I oppose the war on terrorism." Political statements are permitted in a school environment.

WRONG: Making the student change or cover the shirt because it contains a political message, or because school officials, a majority of students, or the community agree with deployment of troops. The First Amendment is not subject to a popularity contest, and in fact is meant to protect less popular views.

OK: Exercising editorial control and screening articles for a school-sponsored newspaper. Because such publications bear the implied message of school backing, officials have a right to filter the content.

WRONG: Punishing a student for distributing publications when they are complying with policy and not endangering the safety of other students or employees. If school officials establish the time, place, and manner in which student publications can be distributed they must stick with it. Unless the brochure or pamphlet crosses the line of being inappropriate, public school employees cannot squelch the message simply because they disagree. The Constitution protects unpopular views. If a student is peacefully giving out flyers and following the school rule, then there should be no consequences.

OK: Reprimanding a teacher for cursing out a colleague or a student. Aggressive, vulgar speech meant to provoke rarely wins First Amendment protection.

WRONG: Transferring a principal who says the K-12 curriculum of the school district is not rigorous. Criticisms that are in the public interest are usually sheltered.

Student Speech

Tinker v. Des Moines Independent Community School District is the single most influential US Supreme Court case on school free speech. The memorable line emanating from the case: "It can hardly be argued that either students or teachers shed their constitutional rights to freedom of speech or expression at the schoolhouse gate." The 1969 case involved Iowa students and their right to wear a black armband in school to symbolically protest against the Vietnam War.

The principle outlined in the case that still endures: To prevail, school officials must demonstrate that the speech would provoke "substantial disruption" of school activities or invade the rights of others. Using that measuring stick, the court concluded that wearing armbands is a form of symbolic speech "akin to pure speech" and that the act was a "non-disruptive, passive expression of a political viewpoint." The court said that a fundamental right of freedom of expression cannot be squelched due to "a mere desire to avoid [the] discomfort and unpleasantness that always accompanies an unpopular viewpoint."

In 1986, the Supreme Court decided *Bethel School District No. 403 v. Fraser*, affirming the school district's right to punish a student who gave a lewd, vulgar political speech at a school assembly. The court reasoned that "it is a highly appropriate function of public school education to prohibit the use of vulgar and offensive terms in public discourse."

The court was also concerned about the academic aspect of the case. "The freedom to advocate unpopular and controversial views in schools and classrooms must be balanced against society's countervailing interest in teaching students the boundaries of socially appropriate behavior," the court wrote.

Two years later, the Court decided *Hazelwood School District v. Kuhlmeier*, a watershed case that lets school districts remove articles from student newspapers and otherwise control activities that are curriculum-related.

Courts need a way of determining whether certain speech is permitted on school grounds and protected under the Constitution or whether schools can place limits. One technique for figuring that out is the "forum analysis," which enables school officials to control the time, place, and manner of speech. The three types of forums are:

- Open Forum: A public place, like a park, that is traditionally used as a place of free public discourse.
- Limited forum: Generally a public area, like the common area in a school. It is not open to anyone, but has been

made available in limited ways and at limited times for certain speech.

- Closed forum: A private space, not used for an exchange of ideas. In fact, the place's purpose would be lost if free speech were allowed, such as class time, school plays, or curricular-related activities.

Web-Savvy

Students generally have broad freedom under the First Amendment to express themselves on the Internet on their own time, using off-campus computers. The results of that freedom include *Out-of-Bounds* web sites or blogs (both containing personal diaries or posted conversations) that can be course and offensive at best and harbor threats to people and property at worst.

The US Supreme Court has said the Internet is a protected free speech zone, calling it "the most participatory form of mass speech yet developed." But there is a wide berth between speech that is offensive, obnoxious, and insulting—all of which is protected—and speech that places the safety of others in jeopardy.

One Pennsylvania student's web site requested $20 for a hit man. The reaction of that state's Supreme Court was this: "We believe that the web site, taken as a whole, was a sophomoric, crude, highly offensive, and perhaps misguided attempt to humor or parody. However, it did not reflect a serious expression of intent to inflict harm."

Another case arose when a Missouri student was suspended for 10 days for a home-based web site that used vulgar language to criticize the principal, teachers, and other things about school. A federal district court in that state ruled that "the public interest is not only served by allowing [the student's] message to be free from censure, but also by giving the students at [the high school] this opportunity to see the protections of the US Constitution and the Bill of Rights at work."

Employee Speech

Over the years the courts have ruled that school employees are not always free to express their opinions and beliefs. Employees cannot be disciplined or suffer negative consequences for speaking out on matters of "public concern." Schools can take action, however, when employees go public with strictly personal concerns.

The main U.S. Supreme Court case is *Pickering v. Board of Education,* which held that freedom of speech—while not absolute—gives employees Constitutional protection if they are speaking about issues of a public nature, rather than those things about which they have a personal stake. Pickering overturned a school district's decision to fire a teacher for commenting on school expenditures through letters in a local newspaper.

For example, if a teacher criticized a building's weak leadership and lax coordination between grades, it would likely be considered a comment about matters of public interest. If that same teacher complained publicly that she thought she was being unfairly targeted for classroom observations and undesirable assignments, a school district would likely be within their rights to react.

But even standing on principles of public concern is not sacrosanct. Employees can still be disciplined based on that expression (like publicly criticizing supervisors) if the district believes that it will impede the employee's ability to perform assigned duties, or the speech will undermine supervisory authority, disrupt the school, or destroy close working relationships.

So when confronted with an employee speech case, the court's analysis goes like this: Is the speech a matter of public concern? If not, the case ends and the employee loses. If so, then was the employee's speech outweighed by the state's interest in promoting efficiency in the delivery of educational services?

The following rulings illustrate the kinds of cases decided by federal courts on this issue.

- A teacher cannot be dismissed for wearing a black armband to class to protest the Vietnam War.

- A teacher can refuse to participate in the flag salute under the First Amendment if she stands silently with her hands by her side.

Teachers are in a particularly special position as classroom leaders. The courts have found that teachers are role models, and when operating in their official capacity become "state actors"—essentially an extension of government power.

For instance, even though teachers may have a free speech right to join students at a student-arranged "Meet me at the Pole" prayer gathering before school, doing so could be seen as official endorsement of religion.

Furthermore, unlike a college setting, K-12 public school instructors do not have a right of academic freedom. Control of the curriculum—both what is taught and how it is taught—is vested with the board of education and the administration. The Court wrote in the Pickering case that "The state has interests as an employer in regulating the speech of its employees that differ significantly from those it possesses in connection with regulation of the speech of the citizenry in general."

The Future

One of the interesting, if difficult, realities of First Amendment Free Speech law is that it is a moving target. As new cases arise the Supreme Court has an opportunity to adjust the line or mark it in a bolder color. Given the variety of people who populate them and the young impressionable students that so many people want to reach, schools are a natural venue for these kinds of conflicts to play out. The key is striking a balance so that education occurs while students and employees exercise their constitutionally protected speech right.

Key Cases

Bethel School District No. 403 v. Fraser, 478 US 675 (1986). This case held that school officials can prohibit a student's lewd speech before a school assembly. The Court reasoned that "it is a highly appropriate function of public school education to prohibit the use of vulgar and offensive terms in public discourse."

Hazelwood School District v. Kuhlmeier, 484 US 260 (1988). This case held that school districts have the power to exercise editorial control over student newspapers and other curriculum-related activities that imply official approval.

J.S. v. Bethlehem Area School District, 757 A.2d 412 (Pennsylvania Commonwealth, 2000). The Pennsylvania Supreme Court held that a school district was within its authority to discipline a student for a web site that made both derogatory and threatening remarks about an algebra teacher.

Pickering v. Board of Education, 391 US 563 (1968)/ and *Connick v. Myers*, 461 US 138 (1983). Together these two cases require a court to first determine if the speech in question is a matter of public concern, and if so, protected by the First Amendment. Once past that hurdle, the second part of the test requires courts to balance whether the employee's interest in speaking outweighs the employer's interest in maintaining an efficient workplace.

Reno v. ACLU, 117 S. Ct. 2329 (1997). This case held that the Internet is a free speech zone, striking down the 1996 Communications Decency Act, which sought to control indecent communications on line.

Russo v. Central School District No. 1, 469 F.2d 623 (2d Cir. 1972). This case held that a teacher can refuse to salute the flag and keep hands by her side.

Tinker v. Des Moines Independent Community School District, 393 U.S. 503 (1969). This case held that students and employees have free speech rights in school, but they can be outweighed if the speech will cause material and substantial disruption.

Millennials Believe in Freedom from Offensive Speech, But This Is an Incorrect Interpretation of the Constitution

Jeffrey Herbst

Jeffrey I. Herbst is an American political scientist, former president of Colgate University, and former president and CEO of the Newseum in Washington, DC.

College campuses should be bastions of free speech. Today, they often seem to be the very places in American society where there is the least tolerance for controversial ideas. Unfortunately, much of the discussion of why this has occurred is based on the ad hoc experiences of a few campuses that briefly gained national attention when lecturers were harassed or prevented from speaking by unruly and, occasionally, riotous crowds.

Systematic public opinion polling and anecdotal evidence suggests, however, that the real problem of free expression on college campuses is much deeper than episodic moments of censorship: With little comment, an alternate understanding of the First Amendment has emerged among young people that can be called "the right to non-offensive speech." This perspective essentially carves out an exception to the right of free speech by trying to prevent expression that is seen as particularly offensive to an identifiable group, especially if that collective is defined in terms of race, ethnicity, gender, or sexual identity. The crisis is not one of the very occasional speaker thrown off campus, however regrettable that is; rather, it is a generation that increasingly censors itself and others, largely silently but sometimes through active protest. Of course, high-level observations about an entire age cohort are by definition difficult and care must be taken in making generalizations. However, to ignore the different view that many of

"Addressing the Real Crisis of Free Expression on Campus," by Jeffrey Herbst, Newseum Institute, April 25, 2017. Reprinted by permission.

today's students have on free speech would be to doom any effort to promote intellectual exchange on campus.

This paper reviews the development of young adults' perceptions of some of our basic liberties. It then provides a set of recommendations to promote free expression on campus that directly addresses the students' concerns. Most notably, the case for free speech will be especially persuasive to young people if it is repeatedly and powerfully argued that free expression especially benefits minorities and those alienated from society. Young people themselves are the best ambassadors for this message. Such an approach will depoliticize the discussion and thereby build a larger constituency for free speech. Absent such efforts, we may continue to speak past each other.

The following pages outline the true constraints on free expression on campus, and propose several steps that must be taken if campus free expression is to be promoted.

- Elementary and secondary schools must educate students on the First Amendment, how far the right of free expression extends, and the opportunities it affords to those who want to change society. Students carry attitudes with them to college so we must address young people when their views on free speech are first being formed.
- Colleges and universities must make an absolutist case for speech to a generation of students who have more complicated views.
- Critically, we must continually make the case that free speech particularly helps minorities and those who are alienated. The failure to understand the precise challenge to free speech has caused, to some degree, the debate over expression to become politically polarized.
- Colleges and universities will have to become much more deliberate about encouraging advocates of free expression.
- In particular, we must find ways for students to become the advocates for free speech for their generation.

Banning Speakers Is the Symptom, Not the Disease

Attention to the state of free speech on campus tends to spike when controversial speakers are prevented from speaking. As dramatic indictments of the core tenets of our institutions, these are moments that make for good press and photos. Among the most commonly cited examples are Middlebury College (Charles Murray, whose writings on race and intelligence have been highly controversial, was kept from speaking and then, shockingly, attacked); Brown University (former NYPD Commissioner Ray Kelly was prevented from speaking); Yale (an email about Halloween costumes became a reason to denounce a residential college dean and a professor); University of California, Berkeley (online provocateur Milo Yiannopoulos was barred from the podium by a crowd); and the University of Pennsylvania (students shouted down the CIA director so that he eventually left the stage).

Yet, there are more than 4,000 colleges and universities across the country and each of these incidents, while awful, does not give us an accurate understanding of the state of free speech on campus. Also, the press tends to focus on elite, highly selective colleges that are in many ways not representative of other campuses (recognizing also that this type of campus may be particularly prone to censorship by the crowd).

The problem with the episodic focus on free speech is the assumption that if controversial lecturers were allowed to express their opinions, the problem would be solved. However, the problem goes much deeper. Charles Murray, for instance, has spoken at many colleges and universities over the years. Are the students at Middlebury who prevented him from speaking in March 2017 uniquely intolerant? They probably are not. Rather, a particular combination of factors (the presence of talented student "grievance entrepreneurs" who could effectively mobilize a crowd, geography of the campus, bitterness over the 2016 campaign) came together to produce a very bad result. Murray himself argues that being chased off the stage at Middlebury was "an inflection point"[1] in the evolution of free speech on college campuses, but there is really no evidence for this. Rather, the Middlebury incident was more like a ship hitting an iceberg in an ocean filled with such dangers. The actual collision was spectacular (in a bad sense), but the dangers had been growing under the surface for a long time. What is visible from the surface is only a partial glimpse of how grim the situation really is.

Similarly, the excellent PEN America report on campus free speech focused, in good part, on discrete campus controversies (notably Yale, UCLA and Northwestern), noting, "While current campus controversies merit attention and there have been some troubling instances of speech curtailed, these do not represent a pervasive 'crisis' for free speech on campus."[2] Yet, the number of speakers thrown off campus is not a good indication of underlying attitudes and practices toward free speech, because much of the free expression that colleges rightly value should occur every day among students. If activists stop chasing speakers off campus, that would hardly mean that the problem has been solved. Rather, campus tranquility might simply indicate that college administrators have perfected the strategy of not inviting those who might incite protest.

[...]

Promoting Free Expression for All on Campus

Eloquent statements of why freedom of expression must flourish on campus do exist. Most recently, my former colleagues Robert George and Cornell West published "Truth Seeking, Democracy, and Freedom of Thought and Expression," which does an excellent job of making the traditional case for free speech in society and on campus. They are particularly persuasive in arguing that, "The more important the subject under discussion, the more willing we should be to listen and engage—especially if the person with whom we are in conversation will challenge our deeply held—ever our most cherished and identity-forming—beliefs."[11]

However, it is unlikely that these promulgations by themselves will effectively address the campus free expression problems. Rather, two steps must be taken if campus free expression is to be promoted.

First, it must be recognized that the shaping of a generation's understanding of free expression must begin long before college. Second, it is critical to address the alternative understanding of free expression that has developed among students.

Elementary and secondary schools must educate students on the First Amendment, how far the right of free expression extends, and the opportunities it affords to those who want to change society. Students carry attitudes with them to college so we must address young people when their views on free speech are first being formed. For instance, the Newseum's educational wing NewseumED is a vital resource for teachers and reaches more than seven million school children in the United States and across the world. It presents history through the lens of the First Amendment, showing how freedom of speech has influenced conflicts ranging from anti-immigrant movements to women's suffrage to gay marriage, protecting both the "winners" and "losers" in each clash. Case studies, timelines and other resources on these historic movements showcase how the free exchange of ideas was essential to the ultimate resolution. In the NewseumED class "You Can't Say That In School?!," students relive the debate over profanity and anti-war speech in *Cohen v. California* (1971), and decide if they agree with Justice John Marshall Harlan's opinion that "one man's vulgarity is another's lyric."

Colleges and universities must make an absolutist case for speech to a generation of students who have more complicated views. The excellent University of Chicago statement on free speech gets it exactly right:

> As a corollary to the University's commitment to protect and promote free expression, members of the University community must also act in conformity with the principle of free expression. Although members of the University community are free to criticize and contest the views expressed on campus, and to criticize and contest speakers who are invited to express their views on campus, they may not obstruct or otherwise interfere with the freedom of others to express views they reject or even

loathe. To this end, the University has a solemn responsibility not only to promote a lively and fearless freedom of debate and deliberation, but also to protect that freedom when others attempt to restrict it.[12]

Some universities, like Purdue, have adopted the University of Chicago's statement. However, other campuses have taken a more conflicted approach. Middlebury President Laurie Patton, whose students ignored her when she implored them to listen respectfully to Charles Murray, made a case for free speech in the fall of 2016 that presents speech as a tool for promoting harmony on campus as opposed to intellectual discovery:

Rhetorical resilience assumes that free speech is not the opposite of an inclusive society, but the way to achieve it. So when we gather together, let's make our conversations authentic and resilient. Resilience is the ability to change and grow in response to our environment. Let's train ourselves to make critiques, and to respond to critiques, in a way that focuses on the path forward together, and allows for honest engagement. We face many structural challenges as a society, and while we cannot solve all of those problems overnight, we can find better ways to address them if we remain resilient and engaged in free and open conversation.[13]

This view is actually quite close to the attitudes of students who want to see free speech protected as long as it is not offensive. While the Middlebury students made their own decision to chase Charles Murray off the stage (and then through the streets), they had not been presented with a ringing endorsement of free speech that would have taught them that speech is protected even if it does not produce honest engagement.

Critically, we must continually make the case that free speech particularly helps minorities and those who are alienated. The failure to understand the precise challenge to free speech has caused, to some degree, the debate over expression to become politically polarized. For instance, the PEN America report notes that FIRE (The Foundation for Individual Rights in Education), undoubtedly the leading national organization that promotes free speech on campus, "is often regarded as libertarian or conservative and is viewed suspiciously by some liberal or progressive students and faculty."[14] In fact, the free speech group has a long history of defending liberals on campus, and Will Creeley of FIRE admits that he has "long been frustrated by the fact that our successful advocacy on behalf of liberal or progressive students and faculty is not more widely recognized."[15]

In all likelihood, the reason for this misperception is that FIRE's (rightfully) absolutist position on free speech ignores the free expression carve-out curtailing speech that is offensive to minorities or those thought to be disenfranchised. Those advocating for free speech are coded as conservative on campuses when they do not address concerns over offense to minorities or alienated groups, issues that are traditionally associated with the left. The case for free speech then becomes politicized and, inevitably, less strong.

PEN America makes the argument that liberal and left-leaning groups on campus should promote free speech. That is undoubtedly correct but probably does not go far enough. Rather, to truly combat young adults' intolerance of free speech, we must make the case that minorities and alienated groups especially benefit from the full exercise of free speech and free expression. These rights are critically important for those whose speech might be muzzled because of their position in the social hierarchy. It is, therefore, critical to argue that multiculturalism can best flourish in an environment where all speech is protected. If the speech of all is not safeguarded, then power will determine who speaks.

Colleges and universities will have to become much more deliberate about encouraging advocates of free expression. For instance, many campuses rightly celebrate students who, through their own initiative, promote diversity and campus harmony. Yet there are very few colleges or universities that go out of their way to honor students who have exercised free speech (except when it is for a cause that administrators believe in). Schools could also sponsor debates that intentionally bring together speakers with different views to show the value of diversity of ideas.[16] Institutions of higher learning seeking to portray a harmonious campus to prospective students seldom talk about the messy discord of their vibrant student conversations. Yet, it is critical to do so if the generational attitudes toward non-offensive free expression are to be countered. Schools also might find that efforts to highlight free expression on campus will attract some idiosyncratic young people who have come to realize how stifling the prevalent attitudes toward expression can be for their development.

In particular, we must find ways for students to become free speech advocates for their generation. Energetic student participation in the Newseum's video contest asking them to explain how they solved campus problems through free expression suggested that there is great potential in having young adults themselves make the case for free speech. Not surprisingly, given their generational concerns, many of the student videos focused on diversity concerns and free expression, addressing precisely the crux of the problem in ways that only they could. We asked the students to produce short videos, rather than more traditional academic papers, precisely so that they could work in a medium that is especially popular with young people.

The Long Fight for Free Expression

Today's young people have deeply formed beliefs that can be traced back to at least when they entered the digital realm. The first step to combating the problem is to recognize that these attitudes need to be countered through programs that, by word and deed, promote a robust understanding of free speech in elementary and secondary schools as well on college campuses. The nature of the programs will evolve over time, but they must make the case that free speech especially benefits those who are less powerful, and we should recognize that students are the best ambassadors for this message. Absent such long-term and compelling programs, the young people will carry the attitudes they have developed into the world at large, making them incapable of fully participating as citizens since not all will live in the self-censoring environments they found on campus.

As Millennials increasingly dominate our society by dint of their demography (they now outnumber Boomers[17]), there is also the danger that their restrictive understanding of free expression will come to dominate our society, to our great detriment.

Notes

1. Charles Murray, "Reflections on the Revolution at Middlebury," AEI Ideas, March 5, 2017. Found at: https://www.aei.org/publication/reflections-on-the-revolution-in-middlebury/

2. PEN America, And Campus for All: Diversity, Inclusion and Freedom of Speech at U.S. Universities (New York: PEN America, 2016), p. 8.

3. Knight Foundation, Future of the First Amendment: 2016 Survey of High School Students and Teachers. Found at: https://kf-site-production.s3.amazonaws.com/publications/pdfs/000/000/228/original/FOFA- 2016-final-2.pdf.

4. The Knight Foundation also asked two questions about speech "that could be seen as bullying others." I have not included the results for these queries because students might reasonably infer from the question that the bullying was directed against a specific individual and therefore might not be protected speech.

5. Jacob Poushter, "40% of Millennials OK with limiting speech offensive to minorities," Pew Research Center Factank, November 20, 2015. Found at: http://www.pewresearch.org/fact-tank/2015/11/20/40-ofmillennials-ok-with-limiting-speech-offensive-to-minorities

6. Catherine Ross, Lessons in Censorship: How Schools and Courts Subvert Students' First Amendment Rights (Cambridge: Harvard University Press, 2015), p. 288 and subsequent quotes on p. 6 and p. 4.

7. Influence Central, "Kids & Tech: The Evolution of Today's Digital Natives," 2016. Found at: http://influence-central.com/kids-tech-the-evolution-of-todays-digital-natives

8. 9 Knight Foundation and Newseum Institute, Free Expression on Campus: A Survey of U.S. College Students and U.S. Adults, 2016. Found at: https://www.knightfoundation.org/media/uploads/publication_pdfs/FreeSpeech_campus.pdf

9. Osita Nwanevu, "The Kids Are Right," Slate, March 12, 2017. Found at: http://www.slate.com/articles/news_and_politics/cover_story/2017/03/there_s_nothing_outrageous_about _stamping_out_bigoted_speech.html

10. He makes clear in the article that he is focused on elite private schools. William Deresiewicz, "On Political Correctness: Power, Class and the New Campus Religion," The American Scholar (Spring 2017). Found at: https://theamericanscholar.org/on-political-correctness/

11. Found at: http://jmp.princeton.edu/statement

12. "Free Speech on Campus," January 6, 2015. Found at: http://www.law.uchicago.edu/news/free-speechcampus-report-university-faculty-committee

13. Laurie Patton, "Rhetorical Resilience: Free Speech and Inclusivity," The Middlebury Campus, September 14, 2016. Found at: https://middleburycampus. com/article/rhetorical-resilience-free-speechand-inclusivity/

14. p. 75.

15. Will Creely, "Reviewing Pen America's Campus Free Expression Report," October 20, 2016. Found at: https://www.thefire.org/reviewing-pen-americas-campus-free-speech-report/

16. I am grateful to John Wilson for this suggestion.

17. U.S. Census Bureau, "Millennials Outnumber Baby Boomers and Are Far More Diverse, Census Bureau Reports," June 25, 2015. Found at: https://www.census. gov/newsroom/pressreleases/2015/cb15-113.html

The Dire Threats to Free Speech on College Campuses

Greg Lukianoff

Greg Lukianoff is the president of the Foundation for Individual Rights in Education (FIRE). He previously served as FIRE's first director of legal and public advocacy until he was appointed president in 2006. He is also an attorney and the author of the books Unlearning Liberty: Campus Censorship and the End of American Debate *and* Freedom From Speech.

There isn't a week that goes by without a campus free speech controversy reaching the headlines. That's why it's as important as ever that we at the Foundation for Individual Rights in Education (FIRE) review the record each year and shine a spotlight on the 10 worst schools for free speech.

Since FIRE's first "worst of the worst" list was released in 2011, the number of colleges and universities with the most restrictive speech codes has declined. However, 92 percent of American colleges still maintain speech codes that either clearly restrict— or could too easily be used to restrict—free speech. Students still find themselves corralled into absurdly-named "free speech zones," taxed when they invite speakers deemed "controversial" by administrators, or even anonymously reported on by their fellow students when their speech is subjectively perceived to be "biased."

The average person muzzled on a college campus is often an everyday college student or faculty member: someone who wants to chat about politics, a student who confides in a friend about their own mental health concerns, or a group of students that simply want to discuss free speech controversies with their peers.

As always, our list is presented in no particular order, and it includes both public and private institutions. Public colleges and

"The 10 Worst Colleges For Free Speech: 2017," by Greg Lukianoff, Oath Inc., February 22, 2017. Reprinted by permission.

universities are bound by the First Amendment, while private colleges on this list, though not required by the Constitution to respect student and faculty speech rights, explicitly promise to do so.

If you believe FIRE missed a college, or if you want to nominate a college for next year's list, please let us know in the comments. Most of all, if you want to challenge your own school's speech codes, please get in touch with us. FIRE is happy to work with schools to improve their speech codes. You can find more information on our website at www.thefire.org.

Northern Michigan University

Any list of schools that most shocked the conscience with their censorship in the past year would have to include Northern Michigan University (NMU). Until last year, NMU had a long-standing practice of prohibiting students suspected of engaging in or considering self-harm from discussing "suicidal or self-destructive thoughts or actions" with other students. If they did, they faced the threat of disciplinary action.

After FIRE brought this information to a national stage, causing a social media firestorm, NMU hastily distanced itself from the practice and publicly committed not to punish students for discussing thoughts of self-harm.

Unfortunately, NMU has not answered all of its students' questions. NMU is currently under investigation by the Departments of Justice and Education for allegations that it threatened to disenroll a student for discussing mental illness with a friend. The school allegedly forced the student to sign a behavioral contract promising not to do so again. Is that student now free from her contract? Is every student who received a letter about discussing self-harm now free to speak out? Will NMU ever acknowledge and apologize to the countless students it hurt in the past, many of whom have spoken up to FIRE and online? Until we get answers, NMU remains on our list of worst schools for free speech.

California State University, Los Angeles

Last February, conservative author and political commentator Ben Shapiro was scheduled to speak at California State University, Los Angeles (CSULA) at the invitation of a student chapter of Young America's Foundation. After students threatened to protest Shapiro's speech, CSULA demanded that the students hosting the event pay the cost of security because the appearance was "controversial." The students objected, but it didn't matter; CSULA President William Covino unilaterally canceled Shapiro's speech, claiming he could appear at some future date if accompanied by a panel of speakers who disagree with him.

Shapiro threatened to show up and speak anyway. Hours before he was set to appear, CSULA relented. But while CSULA administrators no longer attempted to prevent Shapiro's speech, some student protesters picked up where the university left off. Some students did the right thing by protesting outside—exercising a "more speech" response to speech they found offensive. However, other students engaged in a "heckler's veto" by pulling the fire alarm and attempting to prevent attendees from entering the venue.

For all this, CSULA earned a bruised reputation for its lackluster dedication to freedom of expression—and a lawsuit. Shapiro and Young America's Foundation sued CSULA, compelling the university to change the policy that allowed it to impose a tax on controversial speech. The lawsuit remains pending.

Fordham University

At FIRE, we've seen universities offer a number of viewpoint-discriminatory justifications for rejecting student groups' applications to become officially recognized, but few are as persistent and brazen as Fordham University's.

On November 17, the Fordham United Student Government (USG) Senate and Executive Board approved a prospective Students for Justice in Palestine (SJP) chapter. Dean of Students Keith Eldredge informed SJP's members that he wanted to review the group's status before it could be granted official recognition, and then chose to overrule the USG and deny SJP's recognition on December 22. Eldredge wrote that he "cannot support an organization whose sole purpose is advocating political goals of a specific group, and against a specific country" and that "the Israeli-Palestinian conflict ... often leads to polarization rather than dialogue."

On January 25, FIRE and the National Coalition Against Censorship (NCAC) sent a letter to Fordham demanding the university recognize SJP and noting that its reasons for rejecting SJP fail to align with the university's stated commitments to free expression. In its response to FIRE, Fordham doubled down on its rejection of SJP and offered a new baseless justification: that members of SJP chapters at *other* universities had engaged in conduct that would violate Fordham's code of conduct.

What's more, just last week, it was reported that Fordham is retaliating against a student who organized a rally to protest the school's decision to ban SJP. Senior Sapphira Lurie has a hearing scheduled for today with Eldredge—who denied Lurie's request to bring counsel and will conduct the hearing despite being both the complainant and adjudicator.

Fordham's persistent refusal to live up to the promises it makes to its students earned it warnings from FIRE—and a place on this list.

University of Oregon

The University of Oregon's (UO's) Bias Response Team (BRT), and its response to a professor's off-campus Halloween costume, earned it a spot on this year's list.

UO's BRT, which responds to student complaints about offensive (yet protected) speech, found itself embroiled in public controversy last spring and then tried to hide its records from public scrutiny. Criticism arose when the BRT's annual reports surfaced, revealing that the BRT had intervened with the student newspaper because of a complaint that it "gave less press coverage to trans students and students of color." In another instance, UO dispatched a case manager to dictate "community standards and expectations to" students who had the audacity to express "anger about oppression."

When FIRE asked UO for records surrounding the complaints, UO claimed that it wouldn't be in the public interest to share the records and demanded that FIRE pay for them. Apparent suppression of protected speech, coupled with a resistance to transparency, would alone be enough to earn UO the dubious honor of inclusion on this year's list. But that's not all.

Last fall, a law school professor found herself in hot water after hosting a private Halloween party at her home, attended by students and professors, where she wore blackface as part of her costume. According to the professor, the costume was "intended to provoke a thoughtful discussion on racism" by invoking Damon Tweedy's memoir, Black Man in a White Coat.

The costume did, in fact, spark discussion—much of it criticizing the professor's judgment. That's the proper response to offensive speech: more speech. Yet the fact that students and faculty *discussed* the costume was a factor UO cited in deciding it had reason to override her First Amendment right to freedom of speech and punish her. UO's move puts the cart before the horse and risks justifying punishment whenever expression motivates rigorous debate on campus.

California State University, Long Beach

This fall, California State University, Long Beach (CSULB) administrators betrayed First Amendment principles when they closed the curtain on a scheduled campus performance of the satirical play N*GGER WETB*CK CH*NK (N*W*C*).

The university canceled the September 29 performance due to its apparent opposition to the play's deliberately provocative content. N*W*C* is performed by Asian-American, Hispanic-American, and African-American actors who share personal narratives about how the construct of race shapes personal identity while also mocking stereotypes and racial slurs that perpetuate social injustice.

FIRE, the National Coalition Against Censorship, and the Dramatists Legal Defense Fund wrote a letter to CSULB urging the university to protect artistic expression. The letter argued that the CSULB community should not be denied the opportunities for engagement the play provides. The university never reversed its actions, and Michele Roberge, then-executive director of the Richard & Karen Carpenter Performing Arts Center, where the play was slated to be performed, resigned to protest the censorship.

CSULB has a "red light" rating for free speech and a troubled history with protecting students' civil liberties. Last fall, it ended a year-long moratorium on recognizing new student groups that threatened students' ability to associate and organize, so it wasn't hard to find a place for CSULB on this year's list.

Harvard University

Last May, Harvard President Drew Gilpin Faust and Dean Rakesh Khurana announced their plan to blacklist members of off-campus single-gender organizations, including fraternities, sororities, and Harvard-specific "final clubs." Students determined to be members of these organizations would be banned from leadership positions on sports teams and official student organizations, and barred from receiving recommendations from the Dean's Office for Rhodes and Marshall scholarships.

While not a straightforward "free speech" violation, Harvard's actions so severely violate the correlated right to freedom of association that the university deserves inclusion on this list.

Organizations including FIRE and hundreds of students at Harvard pushed back against Harvard's flagrant disregard for freedom of association. The backlash prompted the administration to announce that at least one favored single-gender club would be allowed to operate as long as it pretended it was co-ed. Even more troubling was the discovery that President Faust was willing to characterize freedom of association as primarily a defense for racists, apparently not realizing it was an indispensable tool for civil rights activism that protected the NAACP and other civil rights advocates on more than one occasion.

Earlier this year came news that the policy may be "revised or replaced" by a new committee made up of faculty, students, and administrators. FIRE strongly urges this new panel to shelve the policy altogether, lest Harvard wind up violating freedom of association for a third time.

Harvard last appeared on FIRE's worst schools for free speech list in 2012. It still maintains FIRE's worst, "red light" rating for free speech.

University of South Carolina

What lesson did students at the University of South Carolina (USC) learn in 2016? Even when you do everything you can to avoid getting in trouble for potentially controversial speech on campus, trouble may still find you.

Last February, USC student Ross Abbott and the campus chapters of Young Americans for Liberty and the College Libertarians filed a First Amendment lawsuit with FIRE's assistance after Abbott was investigated for a free speech event for which the groups received prior approval.

In late 2015, the groups planned an event to draw attention to threats to free speech on campus. The event involved poster displays featuring examples of campus censorship across the country. Given that some of their posters included provocative words and symbols, the groups sought and obtained approval for the event ahead of time from USC's director of campus life.

Despite these precautions, Abbott received a "Notice of Charges" the day after the event, demanding that he meet with the Office of Equal Opportunity Programs to respond to student complaints of "discrimination." Several weeks after their meeting, the office dropped its investigation, but it provided no clarification on USC's treatment of protected speech.

Abbott and the groups now seek that clarification through their lawsuit, challenging not only Abbott's investigation, but also USC's requirements that expressive activity be pre-approved and limited to small, designated "free speech zones" on campus. The ongoing lawsuit is part of FIRE's Stand Up For Speech Litigation Project.

Williams College

Last February, Williams President Adam Falk took what even he described as an "extraordinary step" when he unilaterally disinvited author and conservative commentator John Derbyshire, a polarizing figure for his writings on "race realism," from the Massachusetts liberal arts college.

It didn't seem to matter to President Falk that Derbyshire had been invited by the student organizers of a speaker series called "Uncomfortable Learning," which seeks to purposely confront controversial and divisive issues in its programming. Nor did it matter that the group's president, Zach Wood, is African-American, and that Derbyshire had been invited *precisely* so his writings and comments on race could be debated.

While nonetheless making paeans to Williams' commitments to free expression, Falk asserted that "[t]here's a line somewhere" and "Derbyshire, in my opinion, is on the other side of it." In a single, paternalistic stroke, President Falk declared that there were certain speakers and viewpoints that Williams students weren't to engage, and he showed the lengths Williams would go to keep them off campus. Falk has done his students a serious disservice—and earned Williams a place on this year's list.

Georgetown University

Making its second appearance in as many years on FIRE's "worst" list is Georgetown University. As the presidential primary season got underway, Georgetown University Law Center informed a group of Bernie Sanders supporters that campus was no place for talking to fellow students about their chosen candidate. The students were informed that, because Georgetown is a tax-exempt institution, the law school could not allow any campaigning or partisan political speech on campus.

FIRE wrote to Georgetown Law last February, asking it to revisit its policy on student political speech. Every campaign season, we see examples of both public and private colleges erroneously suppressing student political speech because they believe it will jeopardize their federal tax-exempt status. Indeed, Georgetown Law student and Bernie supporter Alexander Atkins and a FIRE staffer were invited to speak on the issue at a hearing before the House Ways and Means Subcommittee on Oversight. Georgetown sent a letter to the Subcommittee pledging to revisit the law school's policy.

In March, Georgetown Law released a revised policy but failed to answer many questions about permissible partisan student speech on campus. In fact, the group of Bernie supporters continued to face resistance and confusion from the law school for the entire election season.

This is not the first time that Georgetown played politics with speech on campus. The university has for years repeatedly violated its own policies on free speech and expression to the detriment of the student organization H*yas for Choice, the most recent example occurring in September.

DePaul University

While few free speech controversies truly surprise FIRE anymore, it's fairly uncommon for a college or university to put four notches in its censorship belt in a matter of months. But if there's any school that could do it, it would be DePaul University.

Here's the rundown:

In April, after students chalked messages in support of Donald Trump's presidential campaign, DePaul warned all students that they were not allowed to chalk partisan messages on campus due to the university's tax-exempt status—a justification that FIRE has refuted on several occasions.

A month later, when the College Republicans invited controversial speaker Milo Yiannopoulos to campus, DePaul attempted to obstruct the event by limiting Yiannopoulos' speaking time to 15–20 minutes and charging the students $1,000 for extra security. When students stormed the stage and disrupted the event, the security guards refused to intervene. When the College Republicans sought to re-invite Yiannopoulos, DePaul banned them from doing so.

But DePaul was not done infringing on its students' rights. In July, DePaul also banned the DePaul Young Americans for Freedom chapter from inviting conservative journalist Ben Shapiro to speak on campus.

FIRE wrote to DePaul about all of these incidents, urging it to adhere to its promises of free expression for students. Unfortunately, DePaul's response did little besides deflect and blithely repeat its illusory commitment to working with students to invite speakers from across the ideological spectrum.

One might suspect that DePaul would think twice about resorting to the same censorship tactics again. However, only eight days after FIRE's first letter, the university required the DePaul Socialists student organization pay hundreds of dollars for security for an informational meeting about the group, because the event could be "potentially controversial."

These multiple acts of censorship, along with DePaul's sordid prior history of restricting speech, led FIRE to ask whether DePaul University is the worst school for free speech in the United States. So it should be no surprise to anyone that DePaul finds itself on this year's list of worst offenders.

Organizations to Contact

The editors have compiled the following list of organizations concerned with the issues debated in this book. The descriptions are derived from materials provided by the organizations. All have publications or information available for interested readers. This list was compiled on the date of publication of the present volume; the information provided here may change. Be aware that many organizations take several weeks or longer to respond to inquiries, so allow as much time as possible.

American Association of University Professors

1133 Nineteenth Street, NW, Suite 200
Washington, DC 20036
phone: (202) 737-5900
email: aaup@aaup.org
website: www.aaup.org

The AAUP is a nonprofit membership association of faculty and other academic professionals. Headquartered in Washington, DC, it has members and chapters based at colleges and universities across the country. Since its foundation in 1915, the AAUP has helped to shape American higher education by developing the standards and procedures that maintain quality in education and academic freedom in this country's colleges and universities.

The American Civil Liberties Union (ACLU)

125 Broad Street, 18th Floor
New York NY 10004
phone: (212) 549-2500
website: www.aclu.org

For nearly 100 years, the ACLU has been a guardian of liberty, working in courts, legislatures, and communities to defend and preserve the individual rights and liberties that the Constitution and the laws of the United States guarantee everyone in the nation.

Bill of Rights Institute
1310 North Courthouse Rd. #620
Arlington, VA 22201
phone: (703) 894-1776
email: info@billofrightsinstitute.org
website: www.billofrightsinstitute.org

Established in September 1999, the Bill of Rights Institute is a nonprofit educational organization that works to engage, educate, and empower individuals with a passion for the freedom and opportunity that exist in a free society. The Institute develops educational resources and programs for a network of more than 50,000 educators and 70,000 students nationwide.

Center for Inquiry
1012 14th Street, NW, Suite 205
Washington, DC 20005
phone: (716) 636-4869
email: info@centerforinquiry.net
website: www.centerforinquiry.net

The Center for Inquiry strives to foster a secular society based on reason, science, freedom of inquiry, and humanist values, where people value evidence and critical thinking, superstition and prejudice subside, and science and compassion guide public policy.

Center for Public Education
1680 Duke St.
Alexandria, VA 22314
phone: (703) 838-6722
email: centerforpubliced@nsba.org
website: www.centerforpubliceducation.org

The Center for Public Education is a national resource for accurate, timely, and credible information about public education and its importance to the well being of the American public. The Center provides up-to-date research, data, and analysis on current education issues and explores ways to improve student achievement and engage public support for public schools.

First Amendment Center—Vanderbilt University

John Seigenthaler Center
1207 18th Ave. S.
Nashville, TN 37212
phone: (615) 727-1600
website: www.firstamendmentcenter.org

The First Amendment Center supports the First Amendment and buildS understanding of its core freedoms through education, information, and entertainment. The center serves as a forum for the study and exploration of free-expression issues, including freedom of speech, othe press, and religion, and the rights to assemble and to petition the government. Founded by John Seigenthaler, the First Amendment Center is an operating program of the Freedom Forum and is associated with the Newseum and the Diversity Institute. The center has offices in the John Seigenthaler Center at Vanderbilt University in Nashville, TN, and at the Newseum in Washington, DC.

Foundation for Individual Rights in Education (FIRE)

510 Walnut St., Suite 1250
Philadelphia, PA 19106
phone: (215) 717-FIRE
email: fire@thefire.org
website: www.thefire.org

The mission of FIRE is to defend and sustain individual rights at America's colleges and universities. These rights include freedom of speech, legal equality, due process, religious liberty, and sanctity of conscience—the essential qualities of individual liberty and dignity. FIRE's core mission is to protect the unprotected and to educate the public and communities of concerned Americans about the threats to these rights on campuses and about the means to preserve them.

The Heritage Foundation

214 Massachusetts Ave NE
Washington, DC 20002
phone: (202) 546-4400
email: info@heritage.org
website: www.heritage.org

As the nation's largest, most broadly supported conservative research and educational institution—a think tank—The Heritage Foundation has been a bastion of the American conservative movement since its founding in 1973. More than 500,000 dues-paying members support its vision to build an America where freedom, prosperity, opportunity and civil society flourish.

National Constitution Center

Independence Mall
525 Arch Street
Philadelphia, PA 19106
phone: (215) 409-6600
website: www.constitutioncenter.org

The National Constitution Center is the first and only institution in America established by Congress to "disseminate information about the United States Constitution on a nonpartisan basis in order to increase the awareness and understanding of the Constitution among the American people." The Constitution Center brings the United States Constitution to life by hosting interactive exhibits and constitutional conversations and inspires active citizenship by celebrating the American constitutional tradition.

PEN America
588 Broadway, Suite 303
New York, NY 10012
phone: (212) 334-1660
email: info@pen.org
website: www.pen.org

PEN America champions the freedom of writers and publishers. Its mission is to unite writers and their allies to celebrate creative expression and defend the liberties that make it possible.

Bibliography

Books

Klinton W. Alexander and Kern Alexander. *Higher Education Law: Policy and Perspectives*. New York, NY: Routledge, 2017.

Sigal R. Ben-Porath. *Free Speech on Campus*. Philadelphia, PA: University of Pennsylvania Press, 2017.

Paul Berman. *Debating PC: The Controversy Over Political Correctness on College Campuses*. New York, NY: Dell Publishing, 1992.

Erwin Chemerinsky and Howard Gillman. *Free Speech on Campus*. New Haven, CT: Yale University Press, 2017.

William Creeley and Greg Lukianoff, eds. *FIRE's Guide to Free Speech on Campus*. Philadelphia, PA: Foundation for Individual Rights in Education, 2012.

Robin DiAngelo and Ozlem Sensoy, eds. *Is Everyone Really Equal? An Introduction to Key Concepts in Social Justice Education*. New York, NY: Teachers College Press, 2012.

Scott Greer. *No Campus For White Men: The Transformation of Higher Education into Hateful Indoctrination*. Washington, DC: WND Books, 2017.

Laura Kipnis. *Unwanted Advances: Sexual Paranoia Comes to Campus*. New York, NY: HarperCollins, 2017.

Alan Charles Kors and Harvey A. Silverglate. *The Shadow University*. New York, NY: Simon & Schuster, 1999.

Greg Lukianoff. *Freedom From Speech*. New York, NY: Encounter Books, 2014.

Greg Lukianoff. *Unlearning Liberty: Campus Censorship and the End of American Debate*. New York, NY: Encounter Books, 2014.

Gregory Michie. *Holler If You Hear Me: The Education of a Teacher and his Students*. New York, NY: Teachers College Press, 2009.

John G. Palfrey. *Safe Spaces, Brave Spaces: Diversity and Free Expression in Education*. Cambridge, MA: MIT Press, 2017.

Everett Piper. *Not A Day Care: The Devastating Consequences of Abandoning Truth*. Washington, DC: Regnery Faith, 2017.

Ben Shapiro. *Brainwashed: How Universities Indoctrinate America's Youth*. Washington, DC: WND Books, 2004.

Ben Shapiro. *Bullies: How the Left's Culture of Fear and Intimidation Silences Americans*. New York: Simon & Schuster, 2013.

Robert L. Shibley. *Twisting Title IX*. New York, NY: Encounter Books, 2016.

Periodicals and Internet Sources

Larry Atkins. "There Should Be Free Speech on College Campuses for Conservative Students, Conservative Speakers, and Liberal Professors." *The Huffington Post*. August 28, 2017. *https://www.huffingtonpost.com/entry/there-should-be-free-speech-on-college-campuses-for_us_59a4144fe4b0a62d0987b0b3.*

Sigal Ben-Porath. " Rethinking Free Speech on Campus." *The Economist*. October 14, 2017. *https://www.economist.com/news/books-and-arts/21730136-attempt-reconcile-protecting-vulnerable-students-commitment-unfettered.*

Erwin Chemerinsky. "Hate Speech is Protected Free Speech, Even On College Campuses." *Vox*. December 26, 2017. *https://www.vox.com/the-big-idea/2017/10/25/16524832/campus-free-speech-first-amendment-protest.*

Morton Keller and Julian E. Zelizer. "Is Free Speech Really Challenged on Campus?" *The Atlantic*. September 15, 2017.

https://www.theatlantic.com/education/archive/2017/09/ students-free-speech-campus-protest/539673.

Chris Ladd. "There Is No Free Speech Crisis on Campus." *Forbes.* September 23, 2017. *https://www.forbes.com/sites/ chrisladd/2017/09/23/there-is-no-free-speech-crisis-on- campus/#2a5dbafb28cb.*

Frederick Lawrence. "The Limits and Freedoms of Speech on Campus." *U.S. News.* August 8, 2017. *https://www.usnews. com/opinion/op-ed/articles/2017-08-08/how-to-define-free- speech-on-college-campuses.*

Eliott C. McLaughlin. "War on Campus: The Escalating Battle Over College Free Speech." *CNN.* May 1, 2017. *http://www. cnn.com/2017/04/20/us/campus-free-speech-trnd/index.html.*

Catherine Rampell. "A Chilling Study Shows How Hostile College Students are Toward Free Speech." *The Washington Post.* September 18, 2017. *https://www.washingtonpost.com/ opinions/a-chilling-study-shows-how-hostile-college-students- are-toward-free-speech/2017/09/18/cbb1a234-9ca8-11e7- 9083-fbfddf6804c2_story.html?utm_term=.43d6c6ebd72d.*

Sarah Ruger. "The Wrong Way to Preserve Free Speech on Campus." *The Hill.* July 29, 2017. *http://thehill.com/blogs/ pundits-blog/civil-rights/344442-the-wrong-way-to-preserve- free-speech-on-campus.*

Natalie Shutler. "The Free Speech-Hate Speech Trade-Off." *The New York Times.* September 13, 2017. *https://www.nytimes. com/2017/09/13/opinion/berkeley-dean-erwin-chemerinsky. html?_r=0.*

Rosanna Xia. "Hate Speech vs. Free Speech: Where is the line on college campuses?" *Los Angeles Times.* June 5, 2017. *http://beta.latimes.com/local/lanow/la-me-berkeley-free- speech-20170605-story.html.*

Index

2/20
1